Jalapeño Poppers
and Other Stuffed Chili Peppers

By Michael J. Hultquist

http://www.jalapenomadness.com
http://www.chilipeppermadness.com
http://www.habaneromadness.com

Dedication

For everyone who has ever eaten
jalapeño poppers and fallen in love with them.

For all who crave to stuff chili peppers with delicious
goodness, but just need a creative push.

This is to all of you!

And to Jalapeño Miss.
Your hotness is beyond compare.

Acknowledgements

I would like to once again acknowledge my wife,
Jalapeño Miss (though she's still also Crazy Patty),
for everything she's done in my life and for this
book.

She truly rocks.

I would also like to thank everyone who has ever
visited our Madness web sites.
You've all been great to work with.
You are the best people in the world!

What's Inside?

An Introduction to Our Collection

Everybody loves jalapeno poppers and stuffed peppers. You'll find them in restaurants, at parties and special gatherings, office meetings, fast food joints, frozen food sections in the grocery store, just about everywhere.

Why?

Because jalapeno poppers and stuffed chili peppers are delicious! Seriously, we love jalapeno poppers and chili peppers so much that we have dedicated an entire book specifically to these delectable treats.

The collection includes more than 100 recipes, from jalapeno poppers to armadillo eggs to stuffed chili peppers galore, along with plenty of creative ideas to help you create new dishes.

Whether you are a seasoned chilihead or just getting started, this collection will work as a jumping off point for creative cooking with chili peppers. Perfect for the home cook who wants more spice in life. Our focus is not only on the recipes themselves, but in bring new ideas to you so you can learn to make an infinite variety of poppers and stuffed peppers. We do our best to keep things simple by using basic techniques and commonly found ingredients, as this is truly geared toward the home cook who loves chili peppers.

We hope you enjoy our collection of jalapeno poppers, stuffed pepper recipes and more. With this book, you're sure to be the hit of the next party. Watch your popularity grow. Throw away all those old books telling you how to win friends and win people over. This book will help you with all of that. Just bring the poppers!

What is a Jalapeno Popper?

Jalapeno Poppers are extremely popular snacks made by stuffing hollowed out jalapeno peppers with something delicious that will fit inside the pepper. It is then typically breaded or wrapped in bacon, and then baked, grilled, or fried, then served as an appetizer, snack, meal, or dessert, depending on where you're from or how much you like jalapeno peppers. Note the word "typical". While there are typical ways to make jalapeno poppers, there are numerous variations.

The typical way to prepare a jalapeno popper is to slice off the top of a jalapeno, and then remove the pepper innards with either a thin knife or a pepper corer. Common recipes call for stuffing the pepper with cream cheese or a mixture involving cream cheese, although you can pretty much stuff your jalapeno peppers with anything you like.

After stuffing the jalapeno peppers with your preferred stuffing, they are often breaded and then cooked. You don't have to bread them if you don't want to. Cooking methods vary but traditionally involve baking, grilling, or frying.

Another variation is the "jalapeno boat" method, which involves slicing the jalapeno peppers in half lengthwise, coring them, and then setting the peppers skin side down on a baking sheet. You can then scoop your stuffing on top of these jalapeno slices, or "boats", and cook them. It is best to bake them with this method, as frying is difficult. Grilling works as well, although the poppers can sometimes tip over if you're not careful. So be careful.

Atomic Buffalo Turds?

Perhaps you've heard of these - Atomic Buffalo Turds is a fancy name for a different style of jalapeno popper. They are basically jalapeno peppers sliced in half, stuffed with cream cheese or other fillings, then wrapped in bacon and cooked appropriately. We use this cooking variation often in this collection, but we prefer the less colorful name of "jalapeno popper". Still, by any other name, they're delicious.

What do you call the same recipe made with habanero peppers instead of jalapeno peppers? Nuclear Buffalo Turds! I suppose if we start making these with ghost peppers, we'll have to come up with something even crazier.

Jalapeno Popper Calories

Ok, so you love jalapeno poppers. Great! But exactly how many calories are in a jalapeno popper? It depends on how you prepare your popper. What are you stuffing your jalapeno with? Are you wrapping it in bacon? Breading it? How are you cooking the popper? Grilling? Baking? Deep frying?

The short answer is that your calories will greatly vary depending on how you prepare them. Typically, other web sites report on the frozen jalapeno poppers you purchase in your grocery store's frozen food section. Based on that, you'll find:

Jalapeno Popper Serving Size: ~3.5 ounces/3 jalapeno poppers
Jalapeno Popper Calories: ~280 Calories
Total Fat: ~19 Grams

The jalapeno pepper itself only has about 5 calories (depending on size). You can reduce the number of calories by stuffing the jalapenos with reduced fat cream cheese or low fat cheddar cheese. Instead of deep frying the stuffed jalapeno peppers, which is the most popular method, try grilling or baking them. You really don't need all the oil to deliver a delicious jalapeno popper.

Cooking and Preparation

Breaking down a typical jalapeno popper or stuffed chili pepper recipe is simple. You'll basically follow these steps:

1. Roast or bake the peppers, then peel them. (Optional)
2. Clean and Core the peppers
3. Prepare your stuffing
4. Stuff the peppers with your stuffing of choice
5. Coat the poppers with batter or breading of choice (if desired)
6. Cook the poppers or stuffed peppers
7. Serve with an appropriate sauce

In some variations, you can roast and peel your peppers before stuffing them, which makes for a great dish. These notes apply to both jalapeno poppers as well as other chili peppers. While some recipes here don't call for roasting and peeling, we recommend trying some of the recipes both ways - with and without roasting. It will make for a fun and interesting experiment to see which way you prefer.

Roasting and Peeling Peppers

Roasting chili peppers allows you to easily remove the outer chili pepper skin and also alters the flavor of the pepper. Roasted chili peppers are delicious and soft, and also perfect for making stuffed pepper recipes. Traditional ways to roast peppers include roasting over an open fire, broiling, baking or grilling. Basically, you apply a heat source, wait for the chili pepper skins to blacken, char, and loosen, then peel. The hotter the heat source, the more you will affect the actual meat of the pepper, so beware of applying too high of heat.

How to Roast Chili Peppers on a Gas Stove with Open Flame

1. Produce a HIGH FLAME.
2. Place the chili pepper directly over the flame. Allow skin to blacken and bubble up. It will do so in about 2-3 minute.
3. Flip the chili pepper and blacken both sides. Do not allow to catch fire.
4. Add chili pepper to a plastic baggie and seal. Allow to steam in the baggie about 5 minutes to loosen the skin.
5. Remove pepper from baggie and peel off the skin. A towel will help, or a fork. Discard the skin.
6. Cook the roasted peppers into any recipe you wish!

NOTE: You can adapt this recipe to the grill by heating the grill to HIGH heat, and roasting the peppers the same way over the heated grill. Again, the chili pepper skin will blacken and blister. From there, move onto step #4 and continue onward!

How to Roast Chili Peppers in the Oven

1. Set the oven to broil.
2. Place whole chili peppers on a lightly oiled baking sheet and broil about 10-15 minutes, or until skins are thoroughly blackened.
3. Flip the peppers to expose the other side and broil another 5-10 minutes, or until skins are thoroughly charred.
4. Remove peppers from heat.
5. Add chili peppers to a plastic baggie and seal. Allow to steam in the baggie about 5 minutes to loosen the skin.
6. Remove peppers from baggie and peel off the skins. A towel will help, or a fork. Discard the skin.
7. Cook the roasted peppers into any recipe you wish!

Cleaning and Coring

Cleaning is obvious, but coring? Hmmm. Easy also! If you don't have a fancy pepper corer, which looks like a long round poker, you can just as easily use a sharp knife. Simply cut off the stem of the jalapeno, then carefully cut out the insides of the pepper, including the seeds. Just be careful not to pierce the outer flesh of the pepper, or else you'll risk some of your popper stuffing oozing out during the cooking process.

Rinse afterward and you're ready for stuffing.

Avoid rinsing if you're roasting your peppers, as you may rinse off the wonderful smoky flavor associated with roasting. If you're roasting then stuffing your peppers, you can slice a long slit down the side from stem to tail, then scoop out the seed pod and inner membrane, then stuff as needed.

Another method is to remove the stem then slice the jalapeno in half lengthwise and remove the innards. You can then stuff the pepper halves and put it back together. This works well with sticky cheese mixtures, but might not work as well with less hearty stuffing. It also works well when wrapping in bacon, as the bacon will hold the halves together.

The same goes for other chili peppers. A corer won't necessarily work with other sized chili peppers, like the wonderful poblano pepper. It is best to simply remove the top of the pepper with a sharp knife, then scoop out the insides of the peppers with the same knife.

Stuffing

Most of our popper recipes call for about 3/4 - 1 ounce of stuffing per jalapeno pepper, but this will obviously vary by the size of your jalapenos. You'll notice some jalapenos are a bit smaller and won't quite hold an entire ounce, but some can get pretty honkin' large! Those are the best ones to stuff if you can find them, but taste is unaffected by the size of the pepper.

You can try these recipes with other peppers, but as a general rule, when making poppers with jalapeno peppers, figure in about 3/4 - 1 ounce of stuffing per prepared pepper.

We've also done the same with our stuffed chili peppers recipes. Again, chili pepper sizes can vary, so plan accordingly. It doesn't hurt to have some additional chili peppers on hand in case you've made too much stuffing. Just keep stuffing those chili peppers! Someone will eat them. If they don't, call me. I'm usually hungry.

If you find that you get a lot of spillage of your pepper stuffing, try this alternate method of coring the peppers - instead of slicing off the stem and coring, slice a long slit down the side of the pepper, careful not to cut all the way through. Spread the pepper open and scoop out the insides with a small spoon or knife. Place your stuffing inside and prepare as normal.

Another way to combat the oozing of your filling is to dab the opening end of your stuffed pepper in a bit of bread crumbs. This will effectively seal up the end and form a crusty barrier to hold in your stuffing.

Batters and Breading

Jalapeno poppers are traditionally breaded with bread crumbs or some type of batter. There are quite a number of breading variations and some go better with different types of stuffing than others. That said, please feel free to mix and match breading or batter styles with recipe variations. You might find a particular flavored beer batter to be more appropriate to your tastes for a recipe that calls for a simple crushed pretzel crusting.

Sometimes you'll find that you have issues with your breading or batter not sticking to the peppers. The batter might run or the breading might fall off. There are some tricks to help you with this.

1. If using a batter, dip your peppers first in flour, then into egg, and then into the batter. This will help everything stick.
2. Make your batter thick. Use more flour and less liquid for your batter and the batter won't run as much, and it will adhere better to the peppers.
3. Try the freezer. After you've coated your peppers with your breading or batter, set them in the freezer for about 10 minutes to harden up the coating. Then cook as normal.
4. Frying typically works better with your breading or batter. Baking gives the coating more time to drip down, so that will be a consideration. Frying begins to cook the breading or batter instantly, making it crispier and helping it stick to the pepper.

The choice is yours!

That said, we've added a few breading and batter recipes to the end of the recipe section for your mix-and-matching fun. Also, like stuffing, the amount of breading will vary based on the size of your peppers. We call for 1 cup of breading in our recipes, but you may need more or less, depending on the pepper.

Cooking Options

You'll also notice a number of different ways you can cook your jalapeno poppers once they are stuffed and breaded. Some options include:

1. Baking
2. Deep fried in a deep fryer
3. Fried in a pan with oil
4. Grilled
5. Wrapped with bacon and grilled or baked

Again, feel free to mix and match cooking directions with different recipes. Note, however, that cooking times will vary based on your cooking method. Baking usually requires 20-30 minutes to finish the peppers. Deep frying only needs a few minutes. Frying in a pan with oil will vary depending on the amount of oil used, and can result in your breading becoming blacker than you might want if you overcook, although the taste is still great. Grilling requires 10-20 minutes, depending on heat level, but up to 45 minutes if wrapped in bacon to ensure the bacon cooks all the way through.

Here are some general guidelines to follow when cooking your stuffed peppers, depending on your choice of cooking:

- Baking: Bake 20-30 minutes at 375 degrees, or until your breading is golden brown, unless the recipe calls for different timing.
- Deep Fryer: Deep fry about 5 minutes, or until breading is golden brown.
- Pan Fried: Use about 1 inch of extra virgin olive oil and fry 3-4 minutes each side, or until breading is golden brown. Be sure the pan and oil are good and hot. Use a lid to avoid splatter. It is best to use a deep pan.
- Grilled: Wrap poppers in aluminum foil and grill 20-30 minutes, or until breading is golden brown, if you use breading, which is not required. Also, you can grill them directly on the lightly oiled grill.
- Wrapped in Bacon: You can wrap any jalapeno popper in bacon for additional flavor and a whole new experience. It might not go perfectly with EVERY recipe, but hey, why not? If wrapping in bacon, bake or grill for 30 minutes (longer if using foil), or until bacon is thoroughly cooked.
- Jalapeno Poppers Wrapped in Meat. Say what? This is a popper variation we'll talk about later called Armadillo Eggs or Atomic Buffalo Turds. Yes, I did actually just write that. Again, more on that later in the recipe section.

You can also cook your larger peppers a bit BEFORE you stuff them. Some options include the following:

- Grill them with a splash of olive oil for 3-5 minutes, cool, then stuff and bake them about 15-20 or so.
- Grill them with oil then stuff and broil them about 5 minutes.

- Bake them in aluminum foil about 15 minutes until soft, cool, then stuff and bake them.
- Or simply deep fry them or pan fry them as needed.

Lastly, you can use a jalapeno griller to make cooking easier. What is a jalapeno griller? There are several of these products on the market, and we even sell one on our site at www.jalapenomadness.com. Basically, they are handcrafted baking sheets with holes cut into them where you can place your jalapeno peppers. The peppers are then able to stand upright while you either bake or grill them. This helps to keep the stuffing from oozing out while you cook.

Chili Pepper Choices

There are MANY chili peppers to choose from. As you know, they differ not only in shape and size, but in heat levels. We have tried to include a number of different chili pepper options for your stuffing pleasure, but again, you can experiment with different chili peppers. For example, a large bell pepper will work just as well as a large poblano pepper in terms of general size, but the flavor will be slightly different. A bell pepper has no heat, while a poblano has a bit of general heat to it - not much, but a little.

A serrano pepper is a bit like a smaller version of a jalapeno pepper, so you might use serranos instead, but note - a serrano has more heat than a jalapeno pepper.

By contrast, what if you used habanero peppers instead of jalapeno peppers? Give it a go! Just remember that habanero peppers are MUCH hotter than a jalapeno pepper. They also have thinner walls and are smaller peppers, so they won't hold as much stuffing, in general. So, please plan accordingly, but make it one of your pleasures to mix and match stuffings to different types of peppers and experiment. You'll love most of your creations.

Here is a list of chili peppers that we personally have found great for making stuffed peppers.

- Bell Peppers
- Poblano Peppers
- Anaheim Peppers
- Cubanelle Peppers
- Hatch Chili Peppers
- Pimento Peppers
- Paprika Peppers
- Sweet Peppers

- Jalapeno Peppers (obviously!)
- Habanero Peppers (small, but bite sized fun!)

Again, we need to reiterate - just about ANY pepper is great for stuffing, though some of the tiny ones can be difficult to work with. The above are our personal favorites.

Sauce Ideas

You don't have to serve jalapeno poppers or other stuffed chili peppers with sauce. They're delicious on their own, but sometimes a sauce will add to the occasion and make your overall meal complete. You can smother the peppers with your sauce, or serve the sauce on the side for dipping. In some of our recipes, we've included a recipe for an appropriate sauce, but feel free to mix and match or serve a preferred sauce on your own. It is always fun to experiment to find the perfect combination.

Other Notes

You can freeze stuffed peppers to soften them before cooking, so if you have a large party coming up and want to be ready ahead of time, freeze your stuffed peppers. Just bear in mind that some stuffing mixtures won't hold up to freezing as well as others.

All that said, onto the recipes!

Recipe Photos

Find recipe photos at our Facebook fan page at www.facebook.com/ChiliPepperMadness or online at www.chilipeppermadness.com.

Jalapeno Popper Recipes!

Classic Grilled Jalapeno Poppers

This is one of the most popular methods for preparing jalapeno poppers - stuffed with cream cheese, wrapped in bacon and grilled. We figured we'd start with the classics.

Ingredients

- 10 jalapeno peppers
- 10 ounces cream cheese
- 10 slices bacon, chopped
- 10 toothpicks, soaked in water for 10 minutes

Cooking Directions

1. Remove stems from the jalapeno peppers and remove innards through the top with a pepper corer. If you do not have a corer, use a knife or very thin spoon.
2. Squeeze cream cheese into each of the jalapeno peppers.
3. Wrap bacon around each jalapeno popper and secure it with a toothpick.
4. Preheat grill to medium heat and grill the poppers for 20-30 minutes, flipping occasionally, until bacon is nice and crisp.
5. Serve!

Bacon and Cheese Stuffed Baked Jalapeno Poppers

This recipe does not include a breading or batter, but feel free to try one out. It is one of the most basic jalapeno popper recipes, but certainly a good one!

Ingredients

- 10 jalapeno peppers
- 2-3 slices bacon, chopped
- 1/4 cup onion, diced
- 1/2 cup mushrooms, chopped
- 3 ounces cream cheese
- 3 ounces Monterey jack cheese
- 3 ounces mozzarella cheese

Cooking Directions

1. Remove stems from the jalapeno peppers and remove innards through the top with a pepper corer. If you do not have a corer, use a knife or very thin spoon.
2. In a large pan, fry bacon, onion, and mushroom until bacon is crisp. Drain and cool.
3. In a mixing bowl, combine bacon, onion, mushroom, and cheeses.
4. Stuff each pepper with the bacon cheese mixture.
5. Bake at 375 degrees about 20-30 minutes, or until cheese is bubbly.
6. Serve!

Crispy Chorizo Stuffed Jalapeno Poppers

This Mexican-style variation of the jalapeno popper can be quite spicy! It is certainly delicious like any other popper, but beware --- these are extra addictive. Try seasoning your bread crumbs with dried chili pepper or taco seasoning in this variation.

Ingredients

- 10 jalapeno peppers
- 5 ounces Chihuahua cheese
- 5 ounces cooked hot Mexican chorizo
- 1 egg
- 1 cup bread crumbs
- Oil for frying

Cooking Directions

1. Remove stems from the jalapeno peppers and remove innards through the top with a pepper corer. If you do not have a corer, use a knife or very thin spoon.
2. Stuff each jalapeno with layers of chorizo and Chihuahua cheese.
3. In a shallow bowl, beat the egg.
4. Dip the stuffed jalapeno peppers into the egg, then coat with bread crumbs.
5. In a deep frying pan, add about 1 inch of oil and heat thoroughly.
6. Fry each breaded jalapeno popper about 3-4 minutes each side, or until golden brown.
7. Top with your favorite salsa and serve!

Bacon, Sausage and Cheese Jalapeno Poppers

This is a simple variation on the first recipe, but includes delicious pork sausage as well for a meatier texture. These are the perfect finger food.

Ingredients

- 10 jalapeno peppers
- 2-3 slices bacon, chopped
- 1 cup pork sausage
- 6 ounces cream cheese
- 3 ounces Monterey jack cheese

Cooking Directions

1. Remove stems from the jalapeno peppers and remove innards through the top with a pepper corer. If you do not have a corer, use a knife or very thin spoon.
2. Slice the jalapeno peppers in half lengthwise, then place them on a baking sheet with the skin sides down.
3. In a large pan, fry bacon and sausage until bacon is crisp and sausage is cooked through, about 10-12 minutes. Drain and cool.
4. In a mixing bowl, combine bacon, sausage and cheeses.
5. Spoon the bacon-sausage-cheese mixture over the jalapeno slices.
6. Bake at 375 degrees about 20-30 minutes, or until cheese is bubbly.
7. Serve!

Jalapeno Poppers - Baked, Restaurant Style

These are the more traditional jalapeno poppers you'll find in restaurants, and the recipe we use to springboard the rest of our collection. This one is absolutely great, and also quite fun to add some variation.

Ingredients

- 10 jalapeno peppers
- 5 ounces cream cheese
- 5 ounces pepper jack cheese
- ½ teaspoon garlic powder
- ½ teaspoon onion powder
- 1 teaspoon Cajun seasonings
- 1 egg
- 1 cup bread crumbs

Cooking Directions

1. Remove stems from the jalapeno peppers and remove innards through the top with a pepper corer. If you do not have a corer, use a knife or very thin spoon.
2. In a mixing bowl, combine cream cheese, pepper jack cheese, garlic powder, onion powder, and Cajun seasonings. Mix well.
3. Divide the mixture among the jalapeno peppers, spooning it into the peppers.
4. In a shallow bowl, beat the egg.
5. Dip the filled jalapeno peppers into the egg, then coat with bread crumbs.
6. Place breaded jalapeno peppers on a coated baking sheet, filled side up. You can use aluminum foil as well.
7. Bake at 375 degrees for 20-30 minutes, or until peppers are heated through and turning golden brown.
8. Serve!

Jalapeno Poppers - Fried, Restaurant Style

Just like the previous recipe, these are the types of jalapeno poppers that you will find in restaurants, only these are the fried variety. This has to be one of our most favorite ways to prepare jalapeno poppers. The breading comes out so nice and crispy.

Ingredients

- 10 jalapeno peppers
- 5 ounces cream cheese
- 5 ounces pepper jack cheese
- ½ teaspoon garlic powder
- ½ teaspoon onion powder
- 1 teaspoon Cajun seasonings
- 2 eggs, separated
- ½ cup flour + ¼ cup, separated
- ½ cup milk
- Pinch of baking powder
- Pinch of salt
- Oil for frying

Cooking Directions

1. Remove stems from the jalapeno peppers and remove innards through the top with a pepper corer. If you do not have a corer, use a knife or very thin spoon.
2. In a mixing bowl, combine cream cheese, pepper jack cheese, garlic powder, onion powder, and Cajun seasonings. Mix well.
3. Divide the mixture among the jalapeno peppers, spooning it into the peppers.
4. Prepare your egg wash by beating the egg whites until stiff. Gently fold in the egg yolks and add to a bowl.
5. Prepare your batter in a separate bowl by combining ½ cup flour with ½ cup milk, pinch of baking powder and pinch of salt.

6. Pour oil into a pan, about 1 to 1-1/2 inches deep, in order to cover half the stuffed peppers when you drop them in. Heat oil to medium.
7. In one more bowl, add the ¼ cup dry flour.
8. Dip each pepper into the dry flour to coat each side. Then, dip into the egg mixture, then into the batter to coat completely.
9. Fry each pepper about 3-4 minutes each side, or until they are a golden brown. The batter should sizzle up immediately when you place the peppers into the oil.
10. Drain excess oil and serve!

Random Tip

Cooking Methods

Most people know poppers as the fried variety found in restaurants, but they can actually be prepared in several different ways, including pan fried, deep fried, baked or grilled. Get creative!

Habanero-Banana Chutney Jalapeno Poppers

Habanero peppers and chutney, you say? Absolutely. Both offer a distinct flavor and in combination they are a wonderful stuffing for a jalapeno pepper. Make extra chutney to serve over the top of the poppers as well. Both sweet and hot.

Ingredients

- FOR THE POPPERS
- 10 jalapeno peppers
- 1-1/2 cup flour
- ½ cup beer
- Oil for frying
- 2 Eggs, separated
- FOR THE HABANERO-BANANA CHUTNEY
- 2 ripe bananas, peeled and diced
- 1 habanero pepper, chopped
- 2 tablespoons onion, minced
- 2 tablespoons fresh lime juice
- 1 tablespoon fresh cilantro, chopped
- Chili powder to taste

Cooking Directions

1. FOR THE HABANERO-BANANA CHUTNEY: In a large bowl, combine all ingredients
2. Stir to combine.
3. FOR THE POPPERS: Roast the jalapeno peppers over an open flame, or use your oven broiler, until skins are blackened on each side. Over flame, it should only take about 5 minutes. In the broiler, it could take 10 or more minutes.
4. Remove jalapeno peppers and transfer to a plastic bag, and seal them up to let the skins loosen. Allow to cool.
5. Once cooled, peel off the blackened skins.

6. Slice open each jalapeno pepper lengthwise with one long slit, then remove the innards with a knife or spoon.
7. Stuff each pepper with the prepared Habanero-Banana Chutney.
8. Prepare your egg wash by beating the egg whites until stiff. Gently fold in the egg yolks and add to a bowl.
9. Prepare your batter in a separate bowl by combining ½ cup flour with ½ cup beer.
10. Pour oil into a pan, about 1 to 1-1/2 inches deep, in order to cover half the stuffed peppers when you drop them in.
11. In one more bowl, add 1 cup dry flour.
12. Dip each pepper into the dry flour to coat each side. Then, dip into the egg mixture, then into the batter to coat completely.
13. Fry each pepper about 3-4 minutes each side, or until they are a golden brown.
14. Drain excess oil and serve with the Habanero-Banana Chutney.

Crispy Taco Jalapeno Poppers

We serve tacos topped with jalapeno peppers all the time, so why not serve them from the inside out? This variation gets your favorite taco recipe inside of the jalapeno for a delicious jalapeno popper. Try it out!

Ingredients

- 10 jalapeno peppers
- 4 ounces cheddar cheese
- 6 ounces ground beef
- 1/4 cup of your favorite taco seasoning
- 1 egg
- 1 cup bread crumbs
- 1 teaspoon red pepper flakes
- Oil for frying
- Sour cream, hot sauce and tortilla chips for serving

Cooking Directions

1. Remove stems from the jalapeno peppers and remove innards through the top with a pepper corer. If you do not have a corer, use a knife or very thin spoon.
2. In a frying pan, cook ground beef over medium heat, then simmer with ½ cup water and taco seasonings, approximately 10 minutes, or until seasonings are absorbed and water has reduced.
3. Stuff each jalapeno with layers of seasoned ground beef and cheddar cheese.
4. In a shallow bowl, beat the egg.
5. Dip the stuffed jalapeno peppers into the egg, then coat with bread crumbs mixed with red pepper flakes.
6. In a deep frying pan, add about 1 inch of oil and heat thoroughly.
7. Fry each breaded jalapeno popper about 3-4 minutes each side, or until golden brown.
8. Top with dollops of sour cream.
9. Serve over crushed taco shells or tortilla chips and your favorite hot sauce!

Filet Mignon and Bleu Cheese Stuffed Jalapeno Poppers

A delicious, medium cooked, tender Filet Mignon topped with melted bleu cheese --- one of our favorite special dinner meals. Think of it stuffed into a pepper! Oh yeah, jalapeno poppers stuffed with filet and bleu cheese will certainly impress your guests, and yourself, too.

Ingredients

- 10 jalapeno peppers
- 5 ounces bleu cheese
- 5 ounce filet mignon
- 1 tablespoon ancho chili powder
- 1 tablespoon onion powder
- 1 cup bleu cheese salad dressing
- 1 egg
- 1 cup bread crumbs

Cooking Directions

1. Remove stems from the jalapeno peppers and remove innards through the top with a pepper corer. If you do not have a corer, use a knife or very thin spoon.
2. Season the filet with onion and ancho chili powder, then grill 3-5 minutes per side for medium doneness.
3. Slice filet into tiny cubes (or mince) to fit into the jalapeno peppers.
4. Stuff each jalapeno with layers of sliced filet mignon and bleu cheese.
5. In a shallow bowl, beat the egg.
6. Dip the stuffed jalapeno peppers into the egg, then coat with bread crumbs.
7. Bake at 375 degrees for 20-30 minutes, or until peppers are heated through and turning golden brown.
8. Serve with bleu cheese dressing for dipping!

Pepperoni Pizza Stuffed Jalapeno Poppers

If you're a fan of pizza, you'll be a fan of this recipe. Pepperoni has a very distinctive flavor and you'll notice it in this recipe, but no worries. It's a great compliment to the jalapeno flavor. Savor this one!

Ingredients

- 10 jalapeno peppers
- 5 ounces mozzarella cheese, shredded
- 5 ounces pepperoni slices, roughly chopped
- 1 tablespoon oregano
- 1 tablespoon dried basil
- 1 cup pizza sauce
- 1 egg
- 1 cup bread crumbs

Cooking Directions

1. Remove stems from the jalapeno peppers and remove innards through the top with a pepper corer. If you do not have a corer, use a knife or very thin spoon.
2. Stuff each jalapeno with layers of pepperoni and mozzarella cheese.
3. In a shallow bowl, beat the egg.
4. In a separate bowl, mix bread crumbs with dried basil.
5. Dip the stuffed jalapeno peppers into the egg, then coat with bread crumbs.
6. Bake at 375 degrees for 20-30 minutes, or until peppers are heated through and turning golden brown.
7. In a sauce pan, heat tomato sauce with oregano, about 10-15 minutes. Simmer longer for a deeper flavor.
8. Pour tomato sauce over jalapeno poppers and serve!

NOTE: Need a quick pizza sauce recipe? Simmer 1 cup tomato sauce mixed with 1 teaspoon fresh or dried basil, 1 teaspoon fresh or dried oregano, and a pinch of salt for about 15 minutes. Stir well. This is quite basic, but nice and flavorful. Add a pinch of sugar for sweetness.

Ham Sandwich Stuffed Jalapeno Poppers

Who doesn't like a quick ham sandwich? How about stuffed into a jalapeno? Then turned into a popper? This turned out great and we're sure you'll love it. To make this one easy, just use some sliced ham from the grocery store. Simple!

Ingredients

- 10 jalapeno peppers
- 5 ounces American cheese, shredded
- 5 ounces cooked ham, diced
- 1 egg
- 1 cup bread crumbs
- Oil for frying
- Brown mustard to serve

Cooking Directions

1. Remove stems from the jalapeno peppers and remove innards through the top with a pepper corer. If you do not have a corer, use a knife or very thin spoon.
2. Stuff each jalapeno with layers of sliced ham and American cheese.
3. In a shallow bowl, beat the egg.
4. Dip the stuffed jalapeno peppers into the egg, then coat with bread crumbs.
5. In a deep frying pan, add about 1 inch of oil and heat thoroughly.
6. Fry each breaded jalapeno popper about 3-4 minutes each side, or until golden brown. Or, skip the oil and bake at 375 degrees for 20-30 minutes, or until peppers are heated through and turning golden brown.
7. Serve with brown mustard for dipping!

Buffalo Chicken Stuffed Jalapeno Poppers

Buffalo chicken wings are great on game day and absolutely perfect with a cold beer. Stuff them into jalapeno peppers (boneless, of course) and you've got MORE than perfection.

Ingredients

- 10 jalapeno peppers
- 5 ounces Monterey Jack cheese, shredded
- 5 ounces chicken tenders
- 2 cups of your favorite buffalo sauce
- Cajun seasonings
- Salt and pepper to taste
- 1 egg
- 1 cup bread crumbs
- Oil for frying

Cooking Directions

1. Remove stems from the jalapeno peppers and remove innards through the top with a pepper corer. If you do not have a corer, use a knife or very thin spoon.
2. In a large pan, fry up the chicken tenders until thoroughly cooked. Season with Cajun seasonings, salt and pepper while cooking.
3. Shred cooked chicken with a fork.
4. Add 1 cup buffalo sauce to the pan and reduce heat to low. Cook about 5 minutes. Remove from heat and cool.
5. Stuff each jalapeno with layers of shredded buffalo chicken and Monterey Jack cheese.
6. In a shallow bowl, beat the egg.
7. Dip the stuffed jalapeno peppers into the egg, then coat with bread crumbs.
8. In a deep frying pan, add about 1 inch of oil and heat thoroughly.
9. Fry each breaded jalapeno popper about 3-4 minutes each side, or until golden brown. Or, skip the oil and bake at 375 degrees for 20-30 minutes, or until peppers are heated through and turning golden brown.
10. Serve with remaining buffalo sauce!

Hot Turkey and Swiss Stuffed Jalapeno Poppers

We love a good turkey and Swiss on wheat bread, but we love it more stuffed in a jalapeno popper! This recipe is great grilled over smoky wood chips. It is also perfect with leftover turkey, so get ready for Thanksgiving!

Ingredients

- 10 jalapeno peppers
- 5 ounces Swiss cheese, shredded
- 5 ounces cooked turkey, shredded
- 1 egg
- 1 cup bread crumbs
- Dippers of choice for serving

Cooking Directions

1. Remove stems from the jalapeno peppers and remove innards through the top with a pepper corer. If you do not have a corer, use a knife or very thin spoon.
2. Stuff each jalapeno with layers of shredded turkey and Swiss cheese.
3. In a shallow bowl, beat the egg.
4. Dip the stuffed jalapeno peppers into the egg, then coat with bread crumbs.
5. Grill the poppers over medium heat wrapped in aluminum foil about 20-30 minutes, or until turning golden brown.
6. Serve with brown mustard or hot giardiniera for dipping!

Bacon and Rice Jalapeno Poppers

Jalapeno poppers are extremely delicious and addicting, as you all know, but when you bring in the bacon...watch out! Cream cheese is a jalapeno popper recipe standard, and quite welcomed, but the brown rice brings in an additional texture and flavor that you will enjoy. Serve these poppers with a simple sauce, like a tart plum sauce or even a plum jam.

Ingredients

- 10 jalapeno peppers
- 6 slices bacon
- 6 ounces cream cheese
- 2 ounces shredded cheddar cheese
- 4 ounces brown rice, cooked/prepared
- 1/4 cup fresh cilantro, coarsely chopped
- 1/2 teaspoon ground cumin

Cooking Directions

1. Remove stems from the jalapeno peppers and remove innards through the top with a pepper corer. If you do not have a corer, use a knife or very thin spoon.
2. Slice jalapeno peppers in half lengthwise. Set onto a lightly oiled baking sheet, skin sides down.
3. In a large pan, fry up the bacon until crisp, about 10-12 minutes. Cool and chop.
4. Add bacon to a mixing bowl and add cream cheese, cheddar cheese, rice, cumin and cilantro.
5. Spoon your cheese-rice mixture onto the jalapeno slices.
6. Bake at 375 degrees for 20-30 minutes, or until peppers are heated through.

Cajun Crawfish Stuffed Jalapeno Poppers

You might not readily consider crawfish for stuffing jalapeno poppers, but it's actually quite tasty, especially with the seasoned bread stuffing.

Ingredients

- 10 jalapeno peppers
- 5 ounces crawfish tails, cooked and diced
- 2 or 3 pieces of white bread, crusts removed
- 1 teaspoon fresh basil
- ½ cup tomato sauce
- 1 teaspoon Creole seasoning
- 1 egg
- 1 cup bread crumbs
- Cajun seasonings

Cooking Directions

1. Remove stems from the jalapeno peppers and remove innards through the top with a pepper corer. If you do not have a corer, use a knife or very thin spoon.
2. In a small pot, heat tomato sauce with basil. Bring to a boil and simmer about 10 minutes.
3. In a mixing bowl, combine bread, sauce, Creole seasoning and crawfish. Mash bread and sauce together.
4. Stuff each jalapeno with crawfish and saucy breading mixture.
5. In a shallow bowl, beat the egg.
6. Dip the stuffed jalapeno peppers into the egg, then coat with bread crumbs seasoned with Cajun seasonings.
7. Bake at 375 degrees for 20-30 minutes, or until peppers are heated through and turning golden brown.
8. Serve!

NOTE: Try different seasonings for the sauce and breading mixture.

Macaroni and Cheese Stuffed Jalapeno Poppers

We've seen a variation of this recipe in restaurants, basically big balls of macaroni and cheese deep fried, and hey, they're pretty good, but when you get it all stuffed into a jalapeno pepper, the goodness increases a thousand fold.

NOTE: We tried this with leftover macaroni and cheese and it turned out just as delicious!

Ingredients

- 10 jalapeno peppers
- 5 ounces cooked macaroni and cheese (choose your favorite brand)
- 5 ounces cheddar cheese, shredded
- 2 eggs, separated
- ½ cup flour + ¼ cup, separated
- ½ cup milk
- Pinch of baking powder
- Pinch of salt
- Oil for frying

Cooking Directions

1. Remove stems from the jalapeno peppers and remove innards through the top with a pepper corer. If you do not have a corer, use a knife or very thin spoon.
2. Stuff each jalapeno with layers of macaroni noodles and cheddar cheese.
3. Prepare your egg wash by beating the egg whites until stiff. Gently fold in the egg yolks and add to a bowl.
4. Prepare your batter in a separate bowl by combining ½ cup flour with ½ cup milk , pinch of baking powder and pinch of salt.
5. Pour oil into a pan, about 1 to 1-1/2 inches deep, in order to cover half the stuffed peppers when you drop them in. Heat oil to medium.
6. In one more bowl, add the ¼ cup dry flour.

7. Dip each pepper into the dry flour to coat each side. Then, dip into the egg mixture, then into the batter to coat completely.
8. Fry each pepper about 3-4 minutes each side, or until they are a golden brown. The batter should sizzle up immediately when you place the peppers into the oil.
9. Drain excess oil.
10. Serve with melted cheese over the top, or with a simple chili sauce for dipping. Or both!

Random Tip

Leftovers

Leftover macaroni isn't the only thing that makes for a good popper stuffing. We've made delicious jalapeno poppers from party dips, mashed potatoes, meatloaf, casseroles and more. Change the way you think. Got leftovers? Transform them into jalapeno poppers!

Vegetarian Stuffed Jalapeno Poppers

You don't need meat to make a delicious stuffed jalapeno popper. You can try a mixture of various vegetables and have a wonderful appetizer or snack. Here's one variation that vegetarians (and everyone else) will be sure to appreciate. This does use an egg wash for the breading. If you'd prefer no-egg, try grilling them without a breading instead.

Ingredients

- 10 jalapeno peppers
- 5 ounces cream cheese
- 1 ounces each of steamed spinach, zucchini, broccoli, green beans, and cauliflower, all finely chopped
- Celery seasoning
- 2 eggs, separated
- ½ cup flour + ¼ cup, separated
- ½ cup milk
- Pinch of baking powder
- Pinch of salt
- Oil for frying

Cooking Directions

1. Remove stems from the jalapeno peppers and remove innards through the top with a pepper corer. If you do not have a corer, use a knife or very thin spoon.
2. Finely chop the steamed vegetables and add to a mixing bowl. Season with celery seasoning and mix well.
3. Stuff each jalapeno with layers of cream cheese and vegetable mixture.
4. Prepare your egg wash by beating the egg whites until stiff. Gently fold in the egg yolks and add to a bowl.
5. Prepare your batter in a separate bowl by combining ½ cup flour with ½ cup milk, pinch of baking powder and pinch of salt.

6. Pour oil into a pan, about 1 to 1-1/2 inches deep, in order to cover half the stuffed peppers when you drop them in. Heat oil to medium.
7. In one more bowl, add the ¼ cup dry flour.
8. Dip each pepper into the dry flour to coat each side. Then, dip into the egg mixture, then into the batter to coat completely.
9. Fry each pepper about 3-4 minutes each side, or until they are a golden brown. The batter should sizzle up immediately when you place the peppers into the oil.
10. Drain excess oil.
11. Serve with your favorite salad dressing for dipping, or a nice mango habanero sauce.

Mashed Potato Stuffed Jalapeno Poppers

These are fun when you want something totally different. Lose the bacon if you want to go vegetarian. Do the mashed potato!

Ingredients

- 10 jalapeno peppers
- 5 ounces cheddar cheese, shredded
- 5 ounces mashed potatoes
- 2 slices cooked bacon, crumbled
- 1 egg
- 1 cup bread crumbs
- Oil for frying

Cooking Directions

1. Remove stems from the jalapeno peppers and remove innards through the top with a pepper corer. If you do not have a corer, use a knife or very thin spoon.
2. In a mixing bowl, combine mashed potatoes, cheddar cheese, and crumbled bacon.
3. Stuff each jalapeno with 1 ounce each of the cheesy mashed potato mixture.
4. In a shallow bowl, beat the egg.
5. Dip the stuffed jalapeno peppers into the egg, then coat with bread crumbs.
6. In a deep frying pan, add about 1 inch of oil and heat thoroughly.
7. Deep fry jalapeno poppers about 3-4 minutes, or until golden brown. Or, lose the oil and bake at 375 degrees for 20-30 minutes, or until peppers are heated through and turning golden brown.
8. Serve with sour cream!

Thai Chicken Stuffed Jalapeno Poppers

The red curry and coconut milk bring a traditional Thai flavor to your stuffed jalapeno peppers. With this particular recipe, you can include more curry and coconut milk than the recipe calls for, reserve it and serve over rice, if desired. This recipe is better grilled.

Ingredients

- 10 jalapeno peppers
- 10 ounces chicken breast
- 1 teaspoon red curry paste
- 6 ounces coconut milk
- 1 teaspoon fish sauce

Cooking Directions

1. Remove stems from the jalapeno peppers and remove innards through the top with a pepper corer. If you do not have a corer, use a knife or very thin spoon. Set aside.
2. In a wok or deep frying pan, heat coconut milk, fish sauce and red curry.
3. Add chicken to frying pan and cook until chicken is no longer pink, about 6 minutes. Reserve the sauce.
4. Shred or finely chop the chicken.
5. Stuff each jalapeno with 1 ounce each of the Thai chicken.
6. Wrap jalapeno peppers individually in aluminum foil.
7. Heat a grill to medium heat and set wrapped jalapenos on the grill. Cook 20-30 minutes.
8. Serve stuffed jalapenos over rice with your reserved sauce!

Thai Chicken with Pineapple Stuffed Jalapeno Poppers

A variation on the previous recipe, but with a sweet addition of pineapple, the dish becomes something different altogether...something totally delicious! You can vary the ratio of chicken to pineapple depending on your personal tastes.

Ingredients

- 10 jalapeno peppers
- 8 ounce chicken breast
- 2 ounces pineapple chunks
- 1 teaspoon red curry paste
- 6 ounces coconut milk
- 1 teaspoon fish sauce

Cooking Directions

1. Remove stems from the jalapeno peppers and remove innards through the top with a pepper corer. If you do not have a corer, use a knife or very thin spoon. Set aside.
2. In a wok or deep frying pan, heat coconut milk, fish sauce and red curry.
3. Add chicken to frying pan and cook until chicken is no longer pink, about 6 minutes.
4. Stir in pineapple chunks and cook about 1 minute. Reserve the sauce.
5. Shred or finely chop the chicken.
6. Stuff each jalapeno with 1 ounce each of the Thai chicken and pineapple mixture.
7. Wrap jalapeno peppers individually in aluminum foil.
8. Heat a grill to medium heat and set wrapped jalapenos on the grill. Cook 20-30 minutes.
9. Serve stuffed jalapenos over rice with your reserved sauce!

Crescent Jalapeno Poppers

These are different from your traditional jalapeno popper, but they were so good we wanted to include them here for you. Try these for breakfast!

Ingredients

- 10 jalapeno peppers
- 10 ounces garlic cream cheese
- 20 slices bacon, cut in half
- 2 can of crescent rolls
- 2 teaspoon fresh parsley

Cooking Directions

1. Remove stems from the jalapeno peppers.
2. In a small mixing bowl, combine cream cheese and parsley. Mix well.
3. Quarter the peppers into even slices by cutting them ½ lengthwise, then again ½ crosswise.
4. Add about 1 teaspoon of cheese to each jalapeno wedge.
5. Wrap each wedge with ½ slice of bacon.
6. Separate crescents into 8 triangles and slice each in half.
7. Fold each bacon wrapped jalapeno into a dough triangle.
8. Place each popper onto a baking sheet and bake 12-15 minutes at 375 degrees until golden brown.
9. Serve!

Grilled Lobster Stuffed Jalapeno Poppers

If you can get your hands on some meaty, hard shell Maine lobster, this recipe is worth the cost. Don't limit yourself to only the tail meat. Try the softer claw meat, and don't forget the butter! We like this one best with a simple beer batter seasoned with seafood seasonings, but it works with traditional breading as well.

Ingredients

- 10 jalapeno peppers
- 2 5-ounce lobster tails
- 1 cup melted butter
- Seafood seasonings
- 1 teaspoon olive oil
- 1 teaspoon minced garlic
- Salt to taste
- 2 eggs, separated
- ½ cup flour + ¼ cup, separated
- ½ cup milk
- Pinch of baking powder
- Oil for frying

Cooking Directions

1. Heat a grill to medium heat.
2. Grill lobster about 6 minutes total, turning occasionally, or until the meat is opaque and thoroughly cooked through. Remove from heat and set aside.
3. Remove lobster meat from tail shells and chop. Add to a mixing bowl.
4. Season lobster with salt to taste, minced garlic and 1 teaspoon olive oil. Toss to coat.
5. Remove stems from the jalapeno peppers and remove innards through the top with a pepper corer. If you do not have a corer, use a knife or very thin spoon. Set aside.
6. Stuff each jalapeno with 1 ounce of seasoned lobster meat.

7. Prepare your egg wash by beating the egg whites until stiff. Gently fold in the egg yolks and add to a bowl.
8. Prepare your batter in a separate bowl by combining ½ cup flour with ½ cup milk, pinch of baking powder and pinch of salt.
9. Pour oil into a pan, about 1 to 1-1/2 inches deep, in order to cover half the stuffed peppers when you drop them in. Heat oil to medium.
10. In one more bowl, add the ¼ cup dry flour.
11. Dip each pepper into the dry flour to coat each side. Then, dip into the egg mixture, then into the batter to coat completely.
12. Fry each pepper about 3-4 minutes each side, or until they are a golden brown. The batter should sizzle up immediately when you place the peppers into the oil.
13. Drain excess oil.
14. Serve with melted butter!

Simple Grilled Shrimp and Cheese Stuffed Jalapeno Poppers

Get the grill going for this easy popper recipe. You don't even need breading for this one, just a few basic ingredients. It's great for a quick side dish or when company just happens to stop by.

Ingredients

- 10 jalapeno peppers
- 10 medium cooked shrimp, thawed, peeled and deveined
- 5 ounces shredded Mexican cheese
- Chili powder or seasoned salt to taste

Cooking Directions

1. Remove stems from the jalapeno peppers and remove innards through the top with a pepper corer. If you do not have a corer, use a knife or very thin spoon.
2. Stuff each jalapeno with ½ ounce of cheese.
3. Season shrimp with chili powder (or seasoned salt if you prefer). Stuff one piece of shrimp into each jalapeno.
4. If any cheese remains, stuff it into the tops of the peppers.
5. Spray lightly with oil and cover in aluminum foil.
6. Grill over medium heat about 15 minutes.
7. Cool and serve!

NOTE: Serve this recipe with a cocktail sauce on the side, although a sauce is not necessary.

Portobello Mushroom Stuffed Jalapeno Poppers

Another vegetarian popper recipe with Portobello mushrooms in the starring role. Portobello mushrooms are thick, meaty, and flavorful. Spice them up with olive oil and garlic and you're in for a treat.

Ingredients

- 10 jalapeno peppers
- 10 ounces Portobello mushrooms, about 2 mushrooms
- 2 tablespoons olive oil
- 2 cloves garlic, minced
- 1 egg
- 1 cup bread crumbs
- Oil for frying

Cooking Directions

1. Remove stems from the jalapeno peppers and remove innards through the top with a pepper corer. If you do not have a corer, use a knife or very thin spoon.
2. Clean mushrooms and remove stems. Drizzle with olive oil and rub with minced garlic.
3. Cut mushrooms into 1 ounce slices and stuff into jalapenos.
4. In a shallow bowl, beat the egg.
5. Dip the stuffed jalapeno peppers into the egg, then coat with bread crumbs.
6. In a deep frying pan, add about 1 inch of oil and heat thoroughly.
7. Deep fry jalapeno poppers about 3-5 minutes, or until golden brown. Or, lose the oil and bake at 375 degrees for 20-30 minutes, or until peppers are heated through and turning golden brown.
8. Serve with soy sauce for dipping!

Italian Sausage Stuffed Jalapeno Poppers with Mozzarella

A variation of the previous recipe, but with the addition of Mozzarella cheese. These taste a bit more like pizza.

Ingredients

- 10 jalapeno peppers
- 5 ounces Italian sausage (about 1 sausage)
- 5 ounces Mozzarella cheese, shredded
- 1 egg
- 1 cup bread crumbs
- 1 teaspoon dried oregano
- 1 teaspoon dried basil
- 2 eggs, separated
- ½ cup flour + ¼ cup, separated
- ½ cup milk
- Pinch of baking powder
- Pinch of salt
- Oil for frying
- 2 cups pizza sauce

Cooking Directions

1. Remove stems from the jalapeno peppers and remove innards through the top with a pepper corer. If you do not have a corer, use a knife or very thin spoon.
2. Grill sausage about 10 minutes, or until cooked thoroughly. Add to a mixing bowl.
3. Break apart sausage with a fork until crumbled. Add Mozzarella and mix well.
4. Stuff sausage and cheese mixture into jalapenos.
5. Prepare your egg wash by beating the egg whites until stiff. Gently fold in the egg yolks and add to a bowl.

6. Prepare your batter in a separate bowl by combining ½ cup flour with ½ cup milk, pinch of baking powder and pinch of salt.
7. Pour oil into a pan, about 1 to 1-1/2 inches deep, in order to cover half the stuffed peppers when you drop them in. Heat oil to medium.
8. In one more bowl, add the ¼ cup dry flour.
9. Dip each pepper into the dry flour to coat each side. Sprinkle with dried oregano and dried basil.
10. Then, dip into the egg mixture, then into the batter to coat completely.
11. Fry each pepper about 3-4 minutes each side, or until they are a golden brown. The batter should sizzle up immediately when you place the peppers into the oil.
12. Drain excess oil.
13. Serve with pizza sauce for dipping, or you can pour the sauce over the jalapenos!

Random Tip

To Roast or Not to Roast

Some recipes here call for roasting the peppers before stuffing, while some do not. We encourage you to try both variations and see which you prefer. Roasting the peppers before stuffing changes the flavor and texture of the resulting popper or stuffed pepper.

Italian Sausage Stuffed Jalapeno Poppers

Get some extra spicy Italian sausage for this recipe. You can season the sausage with whatever spices you prefer, but the sausage alone will bring in some great flavor. Try this as well with leftover sausages from your backyard barbecues. It's a great use of leftovers!

Ingredients

- 10 jalapeno peppers
- 10 ounces Italian sausage (about 2 sausages – you'll probably have some leftover)
- 1 egg
- 1 cup bread crumbs
- 1 tablespoon oregano
- 1 tablespoon basil

Cooking Directions

1. Remove stems from the jalapeno peppers and remove innards through the top with a pepper corer. If you do not have a corer, use a knife or very thin spoon.
2. Grill sausages about 10 minutes, or until cooked thoroughly. Add to a mixing bowl.
3. Break apart sausages with a fork until crumbled.
4. Stuff 1 ounce sausage into jalapenos.
5. In a shallow bowl, beat the egg.
6. Dip the stuffed jalapeno peppers into the egg, then coat with bread crumbs mixed with oregano and basil.
7. Fry jalapeno poppers in a deep fryer about 3-4 minutes, or until golden brown. Or, lose the oil and bake at 375 degrees for 20-30 minutes, or until peppers are heated through and turning golden brown.
8. Serve with ketchup and relish!

Salmon and Brie Stuffed Jalapeno Poppers

Brie is a delicious, creamy cheese that lends itself perfectly to stuffed poppers. The rich flavor nicely compliments the natural salmon oils that all come together with the jalapeno pepper taste. Wrapping this baby in bacon completes the deal.

Ingredients

- 10 jalapeno peppers
- 5 ounces brie cheese
- 5 ounce salmon filet
- Garlic powder, salt and pepper to taste
- 10 slices bacon

Cooking Directions

1. Remove stems from the jalapeno peppers and remove innards through the top with a pepper corer. If you do not have a corer, use a knife or very thin spoon.
2. Season the salmon with garlic, salt, and pepper to taste and grill 3-4 minutes per side over a medium heat grill, or until pink throughout.
3. In a large mixing bowl, combine salmon and brie.
4. Stuff each jalapeno with 1 ounce each of salmon brie mixture.
5. Wrap each jalapeno with a piece of bacon, then wrap each individually in aluminum foil.
6. Grill over medium heat 20-30 minutes, or until bacon is cooked through.
7. Unwrap from aluminum foil and serve!

NOTE: This recipe works great with a jalapeno griller.

Shrimp Stuffed Jalapeno Poppers, Baked with Feta Cheese

This is a variation of one of our favorite Mediterranean recipes. Instead of breading these jalapeno poppers, you only need to bake them with a tomato sauce and chunks of feta cheese. Serve this one on a cool summer evening when the sun dips just below the horizon.

Ingredients

- 10 jalapeno peppers
- 5 ounces raw shrimp, chopped
- 5 ounces feta cheese, chopped into tiny squares
- 6 Roma tomatoes, peeled and coarsely chopped
- 1 Spanish onion, diced
- 2 tablespoons fresh basil
- 2 tablespoons fresh parsley
- 1 tablespoon giardiniera
- 1 tablespoon fresh garlic, minced
- Pinch of sugar

Cooking Directions

1. Remove stems from the jalapeno peppers and remove innards through the top with a pepper corer. If you do not have a corer, use a knife or very thin spoon.
2. Stuff each jalapeno with layers of raw shrimp and feta cheese. Set aside.
3. To prepare the sauce, add onions to a heated sauce pan and sauté about 5 minutes, or until onion is translucent.
4. Add chopped tomatoes, basil, parsley, giardiniera, garlic, and sugar. Simmer about 20 minutes to reduce.
5. Transfer sauce to a large baking dish.
6. Add jalapeno poppers to dish and cover with sauce.
7. Bake at 350 degrees for 30 minutes.

8. Remove and serve!

NOTE: If you have extra feta cheese, top the poppers with it and bake along with the recipe. They'll be extra cheesy, and you'll love how baked chunks of feta cheese turn out.

Spicy Peanut Coated Jalapeno Poppers

Seasoned rice for the stuffing, ground peanuts for the coating, sweet chili sauce for dipping? You need to make this recipe right away! Note the ingredients for seasoning the rice. You can vary this up by substituting in some of your favorite, preferred seasonings, but the ones chosen here make for a delicious combination.

Ingredients

- 10 jalapeno peppers
- 1 garlic clove, crushed
- ½ inch slice root ginger, peeled and finely chopped
- ¼ teaspoon ground turmeric
- 1 teaspoon sugar
- ½ teaspoon salt
- 1 teaspoon sweet chili sauce
- 2 teaspoons fish sauce (or soy sauce)
- 2 tablespoons fresh cilantro, chopped
- 1 teaspoon fresh lime juice
- 10 ounces cooked white long grain rice
- 1 egg
- 1 cup peanuts, finely chopped
- Oil for frying
- Lime wedges and sweet chili sauce, to serve

Cooking Directions

1. Remove stems from the jalapeno peppers and remove innards through the top with a pepper corer. If you do not have a corer, use a knife or very thin spoon.
2. In a blender, combine garlic, ginger and turmeric and process until a paste forms.
3. Add sugar, salt, chili sauce, fish sauce, cilantro, and lime juice. Process briefly to mix.
4. Add rice to the blender and process until smooth.
5. Stuff each jalapeno with roughly 1 ounce of your seasoned rice mixture.

6. In a shallow bowl, beat the egg.
7. Dip the stuffed jalapeno peppers into the egg, then coat with chopped peanuts.
8. In a deep frying pan, add about 1 inch of oil and heat thoroughly.
9. Deep fry jalapeno poppers about 3-4 minutes, or until golden brown. Or, lose the oil and bake at 375 degrees for 20-30 minutes, or until peppers are heated through and turning golden brown.
10. Serve with lime wedges and sweet chili sauce for dipping!

Pesto Stuffed Jalapeno Poppers

This pesto recipe is traditionally served over pasta, but our experiments have produced a version stuffed into a jalapeno. And guess what? It's delicious! If you're feeling ambitious, serve these in bowls over linguini with boiled potato slices and seasoned olive oil, but they work perfectly well as appetizers or finger food.

Ingredients

- 10 jalapeno peppers
- 8 ounces pine nuts, toasted and chopped
- 4 ounces Parmesan cheese, grated
- 2 ounces fresh basil leaves, chopped
- 1 ounce fresh garlic, minced
- 3-4 tablespoons olive oil for the pesto
- 2 eggs, separated
- ½ cup flour + ¼ cup, separated
- ½ cup milk
- Pinch of baking powder
- Pinch of salt
- Oil for frying

Cooking Directions

1. Remove stems from the jalapeno peppers and remove innards through the top with a pepper corer. If you do not have a corer, use a knife or very thin spoon.
2. In a blender, combine toasted pine nuts, Parmesan cheese, basil leaves, garlic, and olive oil. Process until a paste forms.
3. Stuff each jalapeno pepper with your pesto mixture.
4. Prepare your egg wash by beating the egg whites until stiff. Gently fold in the egg yolks and add to a bowl.
5. Prepare your batter in a separate bowl by combining ½ cup flour with ½ cup milk, pinch of baking powder and pinch of salt.

6. Pour oil into a pan, about 1 to 1-1/2 inches deep, in order to cover half the stuffed peppers when you drop them in. Heat oil to medium.
7. In one more bowl, add the ¼ cup dry flour.
8. Dip each pepper into the dry flour to coat each side. Then, dip into the egg mixture, then into the batter to coat completely.
9. Fry each pepper about 3-4 minutes each side, or until they are a golden brown. The batter should sizzle up immediately when you place the peppers into the oil.
10. Drain excess oil.
11. Serve with seasoned olive oil for dipping.

NOTE: Another variation on this recipe calls for coating the jalapeno peppers with ground nuts, such as pine nuts or even toasted walnuts, instead of bread crumbs. If you go with the nut coating, serve with a peanut sauce or perhaps a soy sauce for dipping instead of the olive oil.

Vegetarian Chili Stuffed Jalapeno Poppers

It's fun to stuff your jalapeno poppers with chili and dip them in sour cream. We've included a very basic chili combination with kidney beans, chili powder and cheese, but feel free to substitute your own award-winning combinations. This recipe works great with leftover chili as well.

Ingredients

- 10 jalapeno peppers
- 2 garlic cloves, chopped
- 1 small onion, chopped
- 2 teaspoons chili powder
- 8 ounces kidney beans, drained (½ juice reserved)
- 2 ounces cheddar cheese, grated
- Salt and pepper to taste
- 1 egg
- 1 cup bread crumbs
- Oil for frying

Cooking Directions

1. Remove stems from the jalapeno peppers and remove innards through the top with a pepper corer. If you do not have a corer, use a knife or very thin spoon.
2. In a sauté pan, cook garlic and onion with chili powder and a little bit of olive oil, about 5 minutes, until onion has softened.
3. Add kidney beans to a small bowl and mash with a fork.
4. Add beans to sauté pan with reserved can juice and simmer about 5 minutes.
5. Remove from heat and stir in cheddar cheese. Mix well. Season with salt and pepper to taste.
6. Stuff chili mixture into jalapeno peppers.
7. In a shallow bowl, beat the egg.
8. Dip the stuffed jalapeno peppers into the egg, then coat with bread crumbs.

9. In a deep frying pan, add about 1 inch of oil and heat thoroughly.
10. Deep fry jalapeno poppers about 3-4 minutes, or until golden brown. Or, lose the oil and bake at 375 degrees for 20-30 minutes, or until peppers are heated through and turning golden brown.
11. Serve with sour cream!

Random Tip

Chili Recipes

You can turn practically any chili recipe into a stuffing for jalapeno poppers. Got a favorite? Give it a try. Looking for more? Visit www.chilipeppermadness.com or www.jalapenomadness.com for loads of chili recipes that you can try.

Bay Scallops Stuffed Jalapeno Poppers with Spicy Raspberry Dip

Bay scallops are much smaller than traditional scallops and don't cost as much as their larger cousins. The raspberry dip here is quite simple to prepare, and adds a welcomed sweetness. Also, no breading required on this recipe, but feel free to experiment.

Ingredients

- 10 jalapeno peppers
- 10 ounces bay scallops, thawed if previously frozen
- 1 teaspoon lemon pepper
- 1 teaspoon garlic salt
- 2 tablespoons raspberry vinegar
- 1 tablespoon sugar
- 2/3 cup raspberries
- 1 large fresh red chili, diced

Cooking Directions

1. Remove stems from the jalapeno peppers and remove innards through the top with a pepper corer. If you do not have a corer, use a knife or very thin spoon.
2. In a mixing bowl, season bay scallops with lemon pepper and garlic salt.
3. Stuff each jalapeno pepper with scallops.
4. For the sauce, mix vinegar and sugar in a small sauce pan. Heat gently until sugar has dissolved, stirring constantly.
5. Stir in raspberries and cook a few minutes.
6. Strain and discard raspberry seeds.
7. Stir in diced chili peppers and transfer to a dipping bowl. Refrigerate until ready to use.
8. Heat a grill to medium heat. Set stuffed jalapeno poppers onto sprayed aluminum foil and grill about 15 minutes.

9. Allow to cool and serve with your raspberry dipping sauce.

NOTE: You don't need to cook the poppers as long in this recipe. The scallops don't require as much time and can become tough if you leave them in too long.

Random Tip

Get Saucy

Most poppers will taste even more delicious with an appropriate sauce. You can either smother your poppers in your chosen sauce or serve them with a dipping sauce. Either way, choose a sauce that is complimentary to your stuffing choice. Get creative.

Jalapeno Poppers Stuffed with Dates and Chorizo

A variation of a delicious Spanish appetizer recipe, this jalapeno popper will bring a bit of zing to your dinner party. Serve hot with your favorite drinks.

Ingredients

- 10 jalapeno peppers
- 5 ounces cooked chorizo
- 1-2 slices of bacon, cooked and minced
- 4-6 fresh dates, pitted and chopped
- 1 egg
- All-purpose flour for dusting
- 1 cup bread crumbs
- Oil for frying

Cooking Directions

1. Remove stems from the jalapeno peppers and remove innards through the top with a pepper corer. If you do not have a corer, use a knife or very thin spoon.
2. In a mixing bowl, combine chopped dates, bacon, and chorizo.
3. Stuff each jalapeno with your mixture.
4. In a shallow bowl, beat the egg.
5. Dust each jalapeno with flour, dip the stuffed jalapeno peppers into the egg, then coat with bread crumbs.
6. In a deep frying pan, add about 1 inch of oil and heat thoroughly.
7. Deep fry jalapeno poppers about 3-4 minutes, or until golden brown. Or, lose the oil and bake at 375 degrees for 20-30 minutes, or until peppers are heated through and turning golden brown.
8. Serve immediately!

Heidi's Beer Dip Stuffed Jalapeno Poppers

This recipe is a bit of a variation on the traditional cream cheese stuffed jalapeno popper, but shout out to Heidi for letting us use her outstanding beer dip recipe. These go over great at parties, and be sure to experiment with different types of beer. We're partial to Pabst Blue Ribbon for this one, but feel free to vary it up.

Ingredients

- 10 jalapeno peppers
- 6 ounces cream cheese, softened
- 4 ounces shredded cheddar cheese
- ¼ packet dry ranch dressing mix
- 1 ounce beer (or more if desired)

Cooking Directions

1. Remove stems from the jalapeno peppers and remove innards through the top with a pepper corer. If you do not have a corer, use a knife or very thin spoon.
2. In a mixing bowl, combine cream cheese, cheddar cheese, ranch dressing and beer. Mix well.
3. Stuff each jalapeno pepper with beer dip mixture.
4. Heat a grill to medium heat. Set stuffed jalapeno poppers onto sprayed aluminum foil and grill about 15 minutes.
5. Allow to cool and serve!

Mini Spicy Meatball Stuffed Jalapeno Poppers

The trick with this recipe is to roll the meatballs tiny enough to stuff into the jalapeno peppers, but it's fun to try. The kids will love making them as small as they can roll them.

Ingredients

- 10 jalapeno peppers
- 4 ounces spicy sausage
- 4 ounces ground beef, minced
- 1 small onion, diced
- 1 garlic clove, diced
- 1 tablespoon fresh parsley
- 1 teaspoon olive oil
- 1 teaspoon chili powder
- 1 egg
- 1 cup bread crumbs
- Oil for frying

Cooking Directions

1. Remove stems from the jalapeno peppers and remove innards through the top with a pepper corer. If you do not have a corer, use a knife or very thin spoon.
2. In a mixing bowl, combine spicy sausage, ground beef, onion, garlic, parsley, teaspoon of olive oil, and chili powder. Mix well.
3. Roll the meat mixture into meatballs small enough to fit inside the jalapeno peppers.
4. Heat a large pan to medium heat and cook the meatballs about 10 minutes, or until cooked through. Allow to cool.
5. Stuff each jalapeno pepper with the meatballs.
6. In a shallow bowl, beat the egg.
7. Dip the stuffed jalapeno peppers into the egg, then coat with bread crumbs.
8. In a deep frying pan, add about 1 inch of oil and heat thoroughly.
9. Deep fry jalapeno poppers about 3-4 minutes, or until golden brown. Or, lose the oil and bake at 375 degrees for 20-30 minutes, or until peppers are heated through and turning golden brown.
10. Serve with your favorite hot sauce on the side.

Spicy Indonesian Chicken Stuffed Jalapeno Poppers

Marinade gives this popper an Indonesian flare, and also makes for a perfect dip on the side for serving. Don't be shy with the garlic.

Ingredients

- 10 jalapeno peppers
- 10 ounce chicken breast, shredded
- 1 fresh red chili pepper (use a good hot one!), diced
- 1 small onion, diced
- 2 garlic cloves, crushed
- 2 tablespoons soy sauce
- 2 tablespoons lemon juice
- 1 teaspoon tamarind juice
- 3 tablespoons water

Cooking Directions

1. In a skillet, fry up the onion until golden brown.
2. In a large bowl, combine red chili pepper, garlic, soy sauce, lemon juice and tamarind juice. Let stand about 1 hour to allow the flavors to blend.
3. Add shredded chicken breast to the mixing bowl and coat chicken. Cover and marinate 4 hours.
4. Strain chicken and reserve marinade in a sauce pan.
5. Add water to marinade and boil over high heat, then reduce and allow to simmer about 2 minutes. Remove from heat and let cool. Add in fried onion.
6. Remove stems from the jalapeno peppers and remove innards through the top with a pepper corer. If you do not have a corer, use a knife or very thin spoon. Set aside.
7. Add chicken to frying pan and cook until chicken is no longer pink, about 6 minutes.
8. Stuff each jalapeno with 1 ounce each of the chicken.
9. Wrap jalapeno peppers individually in aluminum foil.
10. Heat a grill to medium heat and set wrapped jalapenos on the grill. Cook 20-30 minutes.
11. Serve stuffed jalapenos with your marinade as the dip.

Spinach Dip Stuffed Jalapeno Poppers

Spinach dip is a favorite among appetizer enthusiasts, and certainly a staple at gatherings. If you've never had your jalapeno peppers stuffed with spinach dip, you'll have to give this one a try.

Ingredients

- 10 jalapeno peppers
- 2 ounces mayonnaise
- 4 ounces sour cream
- 1 small packet dry soup mix (onion works well)
- 4 ounces water chestnuts, drained and chopped
- 5 ounces chopped spinach
- 2 eggs, separated
- ½ cup flour + ¼ cup, separated
- ½ cup milk
- Pinch of baking powder
- Pinch of salt
- Oil for frying

Cooking Directions

1. Remove stems from the jalapeno peppers and remove innards through the top with a pepper corer. If you do not have a corer, use a knife or very thin spoon.
2. In a mixing bowl, combine mayonnaise, sour cream, dry soup mix, water chestnuts and spinach.
3. Stuff each jalapeno pepper with spinach dip mixture.
4. Prepare your egg wash by beating the egg whites until stiff. Gently fold in the egg yolks and add to a bowl.
5. Prepare your batter in a separate bowl by combining ½ cup flour with ½ cup milk, pinch of baking powder and pinch of salt.

6. Pour oil into a pan, about 1 to 1-1/2 inches deep, in order to cover half the stuffed peppers when you drop them in. Heat oil to medium.

7. In one more bowl, add the ¼ cup dry flour.

8. Dip each pepper into the dry flour to coat each side. Then, dip into the egg mixture, then into the batter to coat completely.

9. Fry each pepper about 3-4 minutes each side, or until they are a golden brown. The batter should sizzle up immediately when you place the peppers into the oil.

10. Drain excess oil and serve!

Andouille Sausage Stuffed Jalapeno Poppers

Andouille is a spiced, heavily smoked pork sausage that has a very distinctive flavor. It is a nice compliment to jalapeno poppers, though, and the combined flavors and spices form a little dance in your mouth. This recipe works great with a beer batter, though like all of the recipes, feel free to experiment with breading, or even wrapping them in bacon slices.

Ingredients

- 10 jalapeno peppers
- 1 teaspoon olive oil
- 2 ounces andouille sausage, chopped
- 1 small onion, diced
- 1 clove garlic, minced
- 1 tablespoon parsley, chopped
- 8 ounces cream cheese
- Salt and pepper to taste
- 2 eggs, separated
- ½ cup flour + ¼ cup, separated
- ½ cup milk
- Pinch of baking powder
- Pinch of salt
- Oil for frying

Cooking Directions

1. Remove stems from the jalapeno peppers and remove innards through the top with a pepper corer. If you do not have a corer, use a knife or very thin spoon. Set aside.
2. In a sauté pan, heat olive oil over medium heat and cook andouille sausage about 5 minutes, or until cooked through.
3. Add onion and cook 2-3 minutes, until onion is soft. Remove from the heat and cool.
4. In a mixing bowl, combine garlic, parsley, and cream cheese. Mix well.
5. Stir in the andouille sausage, salt and pepper. Mix well.

6. Stuff each jalapeno with 1 ounce each of andouille sausage/cream cheese mixture.
7. Prepare your egg wash by beating the egg whites until stiff. Gently fold in the egg yolks and add to a bowl.
8. Prepare your batter in a separate bowl by combining ½ cup flour with ½ cup milk , pinch of baking powder and pinch of salt.
9. Pour oil into a pan, about 1 to 1-1/2 inches deep, in order to cover half the stuffed peppers when you drop them in. Heat oil to medium.
10. In one more bowl, add the ¼ cup dry flour.
11. Dip each pepper into the dry flour to coat each side. Then, dip into the egg mixture, then into the batter to coat completely.
12. Fry each pepper about 3-4 minutes each side, or until they are a golden brown. The batter should sizzle up immediately when you place the peppers into the oil.
13. Drain excess oil and serve!

Random Tip

To Bacon or Not to Bacon

A popular saying is "bacon makes everything better". We tend to agree.
Traditional poppers are wrapped in bacon, but not all. As a variation
to some of our popper recipes, try wrapping the stuffed jalapeno
in bacon and then grill or broil them. Use your best judgment.
Not all recipes will benefit from a bacon wrapping, but some
of them might become a new favorite for you.

Horseradish Dip Stuffed Jalapeno Poppers

Ready for some zing? Jalapeno peppers already have their own built in "zing", but pair them with horseradish? Baby, you've got yourself one heck of a combination!

Ingredients

- 10 jalapeno peppers
- 8 ounces cream cheese
- 2 ounces prepared horseradish
- 1 tablespoon milk
- ½ teaspoon Worcestershire sauce
- 1 teaspoon parsley, chopped
- Dash of pepper (or chili pepper)
- 1 egg
- 1 cup bread crumbs (or your preferred breading)
- Oil for frying

Cooking Directions

1. Remove stems from the jalapeno peppers and remove innards through the top with a pepper corer. If you do not have a corer, use a knife or very thin spoon. Set aside.
2. In a blender, combine cream cheese, horseradish, milk, Worcestershire sauce, parsley, and pepper. Mix well.
3. Stuff each jalapeno with 1 ounce each of horseradish mixture.
4. Dip the stuffed jalapeno peppers into the egg, then coat with bread crumbs.
5. In a deep frying pan, add about 1 inch of oil and heat thoroughly.
6. Deep fry jalapeno poppers about 3-4 minutes, or until golden brown. Or, lose the oil and bake at 375 degrees for 20-30 minutes, or until peppers are heated through and turning golden brown.
7. Serve!

Chili Cheese Stuffed Jalapeno Poppers

Normally, when you think of chili, you think of chopping up a couple of jalapeno peppers to get the chili spice level up. With this recipe, it's the other way around. You start out with the jalapeno peppers, and stuff them with chili. And cheese, of course. The standard recipe here calls for 10 jalapeno poppers, but if you make a large pot of chili, you can obviously fill more. Also, this recipe is great for leftover chili (if such a thing exists).

Ingredients

- 10 jalapeno peppers
- 5 ounces chili (canned, or use your own homemade chili!)
- 5 ounces cream cheese
- 2 ounces shredded Monterey Jack cheese
- Salsa to serve

Cooking Directions

1. Remove stems from the jalapeno peppers and remove innards through the top with a pepper corer. If you do not have a corer, use a knife or very thin spoon. Set aside.
2. In a mixing bowl, combine cream cheese, Monterey Jack cheese, and chili. Mix well.
3. Stuff each jalapeno with 1 ounce each of chili cheese mixture.
4. Wrap jalapeno peppers individually in aluminum foil.
5. Heat a grill to medium heat and set wrapped jalapenos on the grill. Cook 20-30 minutes.
6. Serve stuffed jalapenos with salsa!

NOTE: As a variation, you can try this one without the cream cheese. Simply stuff the jalapeno peppers with your chili and continue on with the recipe. Also, feel free to vary up the ratio of chili to cream cheese to your tastes.

Taco Dip Stuffed Jalapeno Poppers

Taco dips are a favorite holiday appetizer, but they're just that much better when stuffed into jalapeno peppers. As a spicier variation, add in some habanero flakes or extra taco seasoning, but this recipe will probably bring just the right amount of kick.

Ingredients

- 10 jalapeno peppers
- 6 ounces cream cheese
- 2 ounces sour cream
- 2 ounces bean dip (or refried beans)
- 1 ounce cheddar cheese, shredded
- 1 teaspoon taco seasoning
- 2 eggs, separated
- ½ cup flour + ¼ cup, separated
- ½ cup milk
- Pinch of baking powder
- Pinch of salt
- Oil for frying

Cooking Directions

1. Remove stems from the jalapeno peppers and remove innards through the top with a pepper corer. If you do not have a corer, use a knife or very thin spoon.
2. In a mixing bowl, combine cream cheese, sour cream, bean dip, cheddar cheese, and taco seasoning. Mix well.
3. Stuff each jalapeno with your taco dip combination.
4. Prepare your egg wash by beating the egg whites until stiff. Gently fold in the egg yolks and add to a bowl.
5. Prepare your batter in a separate bowl by combining ½ cup flour with ½ cup milk, pinch of baking powder and pinch of salt.

6. Pour oil into a pan, about 1 to 1-1/2 inches deep, in order to cover half the stuffed peppers when you drop them in. Heat oil to medium.
7. In one more bowl, add the ¼ cup dry flour.
8. Dip each pepper into the dry flour to coat each side. Then, dip into the egg mixture, then into the batter to coat completely.
9. Fry each pepper about 3-4 minutes each side, or until they are a golden brown. The batter should sizzle up immediately when you place the peppers into the oil.
10. Drain excess oil.
11. Serve with extra sour cream on the side or with your favorite salsa, or even a chili sauce!

Random Tip

Jalapeno Boats

Boat style poppers are a popular alternative to fully stuffed jalapeno peppers. We like them because they are easy to prepare and make for more of a bite-sized appetizer. Simply slice the jalapeno in half lengthwise and remove the seeds and innards, then stuff or "top" and bake as needed. Apply this to practically any recipe here.

Anchovy Stuffed Jalapeno Poppers

Anchovies have a strong, unique flavor that is not too fishy, and the pairing with cream cheese is undeniably delicious. Anchovies aren't only for salads and pizzas. This recipe is a must for anchovy lovers.

Ingredients

- 10 jalapeno peppers
- 4 ounces anchovies, chopped
- 6 ounces cream cheese
- 1 tablespoon chives, minced
- 1 egg
- 1 cup bread crumbs
- Oil for frying

Cooking Directions

1. Remove stems from the jalapeno peppers and remove innards through the top with a pepper corer. If you do not have a corer, use a knife or very thin spoon.
2. In a mixing bowl, combine cream cheese, anchovies, and chives.
3. Stuff each jalapeno pepper with anchovy dip mixture.
4. In a shallow bowl, beat the egg.
5. Dip the stuffed jalapeno peppers into the egg, then coat with bread crumbs.
6. In a deep frying pan, add about 1 inch of oil and heat thoroughly.
7. Deep fry jalapeno poppers about 3-4 minutes, or until golden brown. Or, lose the oil and bake at 375 degrees for 20-30 minutes, or until peppers are heated through and turning golden brown.
8. Serve with a warm plum sauce on the side.

Broccoli and Cheese Stuffed Jalapeno Poppers

Cheese and vegetables have gone together as long as there have been cheese and vegetables. Once you try these poppers stuffed with broccoli and cheese, you'll swear they've always been a threesome. This is a great combo. The curry powder gives them an extra flavor kick.

Ingredients

- 10 jalapeno peppers
- 8 ounces broccoli, steamed and chopped
- 2 ounces American cheese (Velveeta works great)
- ¼ cup sour cream
- 2 tablespoons Parmesan cheese, grated
- 2 tablespoons lemon juice
- ½ teaspoon curry powder
- 1 egg
- 1 cup bread crumbs
- Oil for frying

Cooking Directions

1. Remove stems from the jalapeno peppers and remove innards through the top with a pepper corer. If you do not have a corer, use a knife or very thin spoon.
2. In a mixing bowl, combine broccoli, American cheese, sour cream, Parmesan cheese, lemon juice and curry powder. Mix well.
3. Stuff each jalapeno with your broccoli and cheese combination.
4. In a shallow bowl, beat the egg.
5. Dip the stuffed jalapeno peppers into the egg, then coat with bread crumbs.
6. In a deep frying pan, add about 1 inch of oil and heat thoroughly.
7. Fry each breaded jalapeno popper about 3-5 minutes each side, or until golden brown. Or, skip the oil and bake at 375 degrees for 20-30 minutes, or until peppers are heated through and turning golden brown.
8. Serve with extra melted cheese on the side, or just plain!

Crab, Brie and Artichoke Stuffed Jalapeno Poppers

The stuffing for this jalapeno popper variation is more traditionally served as an hors d'oeuvre, but as you've learned by now, so many dips and spreads can be stuffed into jalapenos and cooked up into poppers. We love this one very much.

Ingredients

- 10 jalapeno peppers
- 4 ounces fresh jumbo lump crab meat
- 2 ounces drained canned artichoke hearts
- 4 ounces Brie cheese
- 1 teaspoon dried onion flakes
- 1 ounce spinach, chopped
- 2 tablespoons garlic, minced
- 2 tablespoons olive oil
- 2 tablespoons white wine
- 2 tablespoons heavy cream
- 1 tablespoon fresh parsley, finely chopped
- 1 tablespoon fresh tarragon, finely chopped
- 2 tablespoons Dijon mustard
- Hot sauce to taste
- 1 egg
- 1 cup bread crumbs
- Oil for frying

Cooking Directions

1. Remove stems from the jalapeno peppers and remove innards through the top with a pepper corer. If you do not have a corer, use a knife or very thin spoon.

2. In a blender, combine crab meat, artichoke hearts, Brie, onion flakes, spinach, olive oil (2 tablespoons), garlic, white wine, heavy cream, parsley, tarragon, mustard and hot sauce to taste. Process until fairly smooth.
3. Stuff each jalapeno with your Crab, Artichoke and Brie combination.
4. In a shallow bowl, beat the egg.
5. Dip the stuffed jalapeno peppers into the egg, then coat with bread crumbs.
6. In a deep frying pan, add about 1 inch of oil and heat thoroughly.
7. Fry each breaded jalapeno popper about 3-5 minutes each side, or until golden brown. Or, skip the oil and bake at 375 degrees for 20-30 minutes, or until peppers are heated through and turning golden brown.
8. Serve!

Random Tip

Make Poppers Ahead

Getting ready for a party? Got lots of guests coming?
Jalapeno Poppers are popular for more than just taste.
They're easy to make ahead of time. Just prepare the peppers
and stuff as needed, then refrigerate until the party starts.
Pop them in the oven and serve.

Ricotta Stuffed Jalapeno Peppers

The key to this recipe is roasting the jalapeno peppers first, then stuffing with your ricotta cheese mixture. Serve these at room temperature for a wonderful appetizer.

Ingredients

- 10 jalapeno peppers
- 8 ounces ricotta cheese
- 2 ounces Parmesan cheese, grated
- 1 tablespoon green onion, finely diced
- Salt and pepper to taste
- 8 large fresh basil leaves, chopped
- 1 teaspoon fresh parsley, chopped
- 1 tablespoon water
- 3 tablespoons olive oil
- 1 clove garlic, minced
- 2 ounces walnuts, crushed

Cooking Directions

1. Roast the jalapeno peppers over direct flame to blacken the skins, ensuring to char each side. Transfer jalapenos to a plastic bag and seal, or to a bowl and cover. Allow to steam to loosen the skins.
2. Once peppers are cooled, peel off the blackened skins. Slice a long slit down the side of the peppers from stem to end and scoop out insides. Set peppers aside.
3. In a mixing bowl, add ricotta cheese and whisk until fluffy.
4. Add Parmesan cheese, green onion, salt and pepper to taste. Mix well.
5. Stuff each roasted jalapeno pepper with the ricotta mixture.
6. To a food processor, add basil, parsley, water and garlic. Process until finely chopped.
7. Add olive oil in a stream while processing to form a puree.
8. Drizzle puree over jalapeno peppers, then top with crushed walnuts.
9. Serve!

Jalapeno Popper Dip

This is not technically a jalapeno popper recipe, but it is quite delicious nonetheless. We just had to include it in this collection of recipes because...well, it's just so jalapeno popper-ish!

Ingredients

- 4 jalapeno peppers, diced
- 16 ounces cream cheese, room temperature
- 1 cup mayonnaise
- 1 cup shredded Mexican cheese
- 1 cup Parmesan cheese
- 1 cup bread crumbs
- ½ stick butter, melted

Cooking Directions

1. In a food processor add jalapeno peppers, cream cheese, mayonnaise, Mexican cheese, and ½ cup of the Parmesan cheese. Process until smooth.
2. Spread dip into an oiled baking dish.
3. In a mixing bowl, combine bread crumbs and ½ cup Parmesan cheese. Mix well.
4. Pour melted butter over bread crumb mixture and mix.
5. Sprinkle bread crumb mixture over dip.
6. Bake at 375 degrees about 20 minutes, until topping is lightly browned.
7. Serve with your favorite crackers or chips!

Chocolate Covered, Peanut Butter Filled Jalapenos (or, Jalapeno Happiness Dessert)

OK, this was a FUN experiment. We knew we'd like it, but Jalapeno Miss REALLY loved this one. It is very sweet and tasty with a bit of the jalapeno heat, though not as much as normal because the insides are removed. It's reminiscent of Bumps on a Log, but infinitely better. Note that these are extremely easy to prepare. If you're in a pinch and you need to whip up some fun desserts for your guests, this recipe is for you.

Ingredients

- 4 jalapeno peppers
- 4 ounces peanut butter
- 1 cup milk chocolate chips
- 1 teaspoon sugar
- 1 teaspoon milk
- 1 teaspoon chili powder (or three)

Cooking Directions

1. Core the jalapeno peppers by cutting off the stems and hollowing out the insides.
2. Stuff each jalapeno with 1 ounce of peanut butter. Amount of peanut butter you can fit will vary per pepper.
3. Heat a small pot to medium heat. Add chocolate chips, sugar, milk and chili powder. Stir until chocolate melts and combines with other ingredients.
4. Set stuffed jalapeno peppers on a plate and drizzle chocolate over them until they are thickly coated.
5. Allow to cool and serve!

Armadillo Eggs Recipes

Armadillo Eggs are basically jalapeno poppers wrapped in ground meat, then baked or grilled to delicious perfection. Looking at them, you can see why they might be called Armadillo Eggs, as they resemble the coarse shells of those tiny creatures. Put your mind at ease. Armadillos are mammals and don't lay eggs. But these are delicious!

The variations are truly endless as you can choose any of the popper recipes previously used here, or make up your own, and wrap them in any combination of ground meat of your choosing. You can also combine the ground meats and season with your favorite seasonings, and serve them with an endless variety of sauces as well.

Also, you don't necessarily need to use an entire jalapeno pepper. You can wrap the meat around halved or quartered peppers and proceed as normal. For an average sized jalapeno pepper, figure that you'll need about 3 ounces of meet to completely wrap the pepper. However, as with any popper recipe, amounts will vary depending on the size of the jalapeno and your preferred thickness of the outer meat casing.

Of course not every combination will work as well as others, so we have provided some of our favorite Armadillo Egg recipes that have served us well over the years. All of our Armadillo Egg recipes call for a whole jalapeno for ease of production, but proceed as you need.

Sausage Armadillo Eggs

Typical Armadillo Eggs are prepared with ground pork sausage for the outer shell and a cream cheese/cheddar cheese combination for the stuffing. You can't go wrong with this version.

Ingredients

- 10 jalapeno peppers
- 2 pounds ground pork sausage
- 5 ounces cream cheese
- 5 ounces cheddar cheese, shredded
- 1 teaspoon garlic, minced
- Salt and pepper to taste

Cooking Directions

1. Remove stems from the jalapeno peppers and remove innards through the top with a pepper corer. If you do not have a corer, use a knife or very thin spoon.
2. In a mixing bowl, combine cream cheese, cheddar cheese, garlic, and salt and pepper to taste. Mix well.
3. Stuff about 1 ounce of your cheese mixture into each jalapeno pepper.
4. Divide the ground pork into 10 equal sizes patties and flatten with your hands. They should be just about 3 ounces each.
5. Mold one pork sausage patty around each jalapeno popper. Be sure to fully enclose the popper in the sausage. Set onto a lightly oiled baking dish.
6. Preheat oven to 350 degrees.
7. Bake the Armadillo Eggs about 20-25 minutes, or until the meat is cooked through.
8. Serve!

Turkey Armadillo Eggs

This version of delicious Armadillo Eggs uses seasoned ground turkey as the casing and a simple variation on traditional cream cheese filling. This version is also a bit lighter and lower in calories.

Ingredients

- 10 jalapeno peppers
- 2 pounds ground turkey
- 1 egg, beaten
- 1/4 cup bread crumbs
- 10 ounces light cream cheese
- 1 teaspoon garlic, minced
- 1 teaspoon cayenne powder
- Salt and pepper to taste

Cooking Directions

1. Remove stems from the jalapeno peppers and remove innards through the top with a pepper corer. If you do not have a corer, use a knife or very thin spoon.
2. In a mixing bowl, combine cream cheese, cayenne, garlic, and salt and pepper to taste. Mix well.
3. Stuff about 1 ounce of your cheese mixture into each jalapeno pepper.
4. In a separate mixing bowl, combine ground turkey, egg and bread crumbs. Hand mix, but do not over mix.
5. Divide the ground turkey into 10 equal sizes patties and flatten with your hands. They should be just about 3 ounces each.
6. Mold one turkey patty around each jalapeno popper. Be sure to fully enclose the popper in the meat. Set onto a lightly oiled baking dish.
7. Preheat oven to 350 degrees.
8. Bake the Armadillo Eggs about 20-25 minutes, or until the meat is cooked through.
9. Serve!

Turkey Armadillo Eggs with Roasted Pepper Sauce

Here we offer a spicier and more seasoned version of our Turkey Armadillo Eggs, served with a powerful roasted pepper sauce that pairs nicely. You can serve these as a meal with a side of your favorite vegetables.

Ingredients

- 10 jalapeno peppers
- 2 pounds ground turkey
- 1 egg, beaten
- 1/4 cup bread crumbs
- 1 tablespoon Cajun seasonings
- 1/4 cup fresh basil leaves, coarsely chopped
- 10 ounces light cream cheese
- 1 teaspoon garlic, minced
- 1 teaspoon cayenne powder
- Salt and pepper to taste
- 4 cups Roasted Red Pepper Sauce (recipe below)

Cooking Directions

1. Remove stems from the jalapeno peppers and remove innards through the top with a pepper corer. If you do not have a corer, use a knife or very thin spoon.
2. In a mixing bowl, combine cream cheese, cayenne, garlic, and salt and pepper to taste. Mix well.
3. Stuff about 1 ounce of your cheese mixture into each jalapeno pepper.
4. In a separate mixing bowl, combine ground turkey, egg, bread crumbs, Cajun seasonings and chopped basil leaves. Hand mix, but do not over mix.
5. Divide the ground turkey into 10 equal sizes patties and flatten with your hands. They should be just about 3 ounces each.

6. Mold one turkey patty around each jalapeno popper. Be sure to fully enclose the popper in the meat. Set onto a lightly oiled baking dish.
7. Pour about 2 cup of the Roasted Red Pepper Sauce over the top of the Armadillo Eggs.
8. Preheat oven to 350 degrees.
9. Bake the Armadillo Eggs about 20-25 minutes, or until the meat is cooked through.
10. Serve with remaining Roasted Red Pepper Sauce!

Roasted Red Pepper Sauce Recipe

We use this sauce with pasta as a substitution for traditional tomato sauce as well.

Ingredients

- 4 red bell peppers, chopped, seeded and roasted
- 10 Roma tomatoes, blanched, peeled and seeded
- 1 fresh Spanish onion, chopped
- 2 bay leaves
- 1/4 cup fresh basil, coarsely chopped
- Habanero or chili pepper powder if desired
- 1 teaspoon olive oil
- 1 cup chicken broth
- 1 pinch sugar
- Salt to taste

Cooking Directions

1. To a food processor, add roasted red pepper, tomato, onion, bay leaves, basil, salt and chili powder.
2. Process about 1 minute to form a paste, roughly the texture of a thick salsa.
3. Heat a sauce pan to medium heat.
4. Strain out extra liquids and transfer to the heated sauce pan with olive oil.
5. Cook paste for 10 minutes and add chicken broth and sugar.
6. Simmer for 20 minutes until slightly reduced.

Beefy Armadillo Eggs

This version of delicious Armadillo Eggs uses seasoned ground beef as the casing and a simple variation on traditional cream cheese filling. It's a bit like a spicy stuffed burger recipe, which we greatly enjoy. You don't need a bun here!

Ingredients

- 10 jalapeno peppers
- 2 pounds ground beef
- 1 egg, beaten
- 1/4 cup Italian style bread crumbs
- 1 tablespoon dried oregano
- 5 ounces cream cheese
- 5 ounces mozzarella cheese, shredded
- 1 teaspoon garlic, minced
- Salt and pepper to taste

Cooking Directions

1. Remove stems from the jalapeno peppers and remove innards through the top with a pepper corer. If you do not have a corer, use a knife or very thin spoon.
2. In a mixing bowl, combine cream cheese, mozzarella cheese, garlic, and salt and pepper to taste. Mix well.
3. Stuff about 1 ounce of your cheese mixture into each jalapeno pepper.
4. In a separate mixing bowl, combine ground beef, egg, dried oregano and bread crumbs. Hand mix, but do not over mix.
5. Divide the ground meat into 10 equal sizes patties and flatten with your hands. They should be just about 3 ounces each.
6. Mold one beef patty around each jalapeno popper. Be sure to fully enclose the popper in the meat. Set onto a lightly oiled baking dish.
7. Preheat oven to 350 degrees.
8. Bake the Armadillo Eggs about 20-25 minutes, or until the meat is cooked through.
9. Serve!

Beef and Cheddar Armadillo Eggs Overload

Yes, these Armadillo Eggs are on cheddar cheese overload, but that's not a bad thing. Plenty of cheddar cheese stuffed into a jalapeno pepper, covered with beef then topped with melted cheese. It's a bit like a spicy cheeseburger, only without the bun, and much more fun.

Ingredients

- 10 jalapeno peppers
- 2 pounds ground beef
- 1 teaspoon olive oil
- 1 tablespoon garlic, minced
- 1 tablespoon onion, minced
- 10 ounces cheddar cheese
- 10 small cheddar cheese slices
- Salt and pepper to taste

Cooking Directions

1. Remove stems from the jalapeno peppers and remove innards through the top with a pepper corer. If you do not have a corer, use a knife or very thin spoon.
2. Stuff about 1 ounce of cheddar cheese into each jalapeno pepper.
3. In a mixing bowl, combine ground beef, olive oil, garlic, onion and salt and pepper to taste. Hand mix, but do not over mix.
4. Divide the ground meat into 10 equal sizes patties and flatten with your hands. They should be just about 3 ounces each.
5. Mold one beef patty around each jalapeno popper. Be sure to fully enclose the popper in the meat. Set onto a lightly oiled baking dish.
6. Preheat oven to 350 degrees.
7. Bake the Armadillo Eggs about 20-25 minutes, or until the meat is cooked through.
8. Top each Armadillo Egg with 1 slice of cheddar cheese. Bake another 2-3 minutes, or until cheese on top is melted.
9. Serve!

Chili Smothered Armadillo Eggs

This Armadillo Eggs recipe incorporates equal parts beef and pork for the casing, then tops them with chili of your choice. It's a great way to use up any leftover chili from when you've cooked up a huge pot for the weekend.

Ingredients

- 10 jalapeno peppers
- 1 pound ground beef
- 1 pound ground pork
- 1 egg, beaten
- 1/4 cup bread crumbs
- 1 tablespoon fresh garlic, minced
- 10 ounces cream cheese
- 1 teaspoon chili powder
- Salt and pepper to taste
- Chili for serving (5-10 cups, or 1/2 to 1 cup per Armadillo Egg)
- Grated cheddar cheese for serving
- Sour cream for serving
- Diced scallions for serving

Cooking Directions

1. Remove stems from the jalapeno peppers and remove innards through the top with a pepper corer. If you do not have a corer, use a knife or very thin spoon.
2. In a mixing bowl, combine cream cheese, chili powder and salt and pepper to taste. Mix well.
3. Stuff about 1 ounce of your cheese mixture into each jalapeno pepper.
4. In a separate mixing bowl, combine ground beef, ground pork, garlic, egg and bread crumbs. Hand mix, but do not over mix.

5. Divide the ground meat into 10 equal sizes patties and flatten with your hands. They should be just about 3 ounces each.
6. Mold one meat patty around each jalapeno popper. Be sure to fully enclose the popper in the meat. Set onto a lightly oiled baking dish.
7. Preheat oven to 350 degrees.
8. Bake the Armadillo Eggs about 20-25 minutes, or until the meat is cooked through.
9. Top with 1/2 to 1 cup of your favorite chili and sprinkle with grated cheddar cheese and scallions.
10. Serve with sour cream on the side.

NOTE: For some great chili recipes, visit our site at ChiliPepperMadness.com. We have quite a few.

Random Tip

Mix and Match Your Meat

Do you have a favorite meatloaf or meatball recipe that includes different types of ground meats? Many such recipes call for a mixture such as veal and beef or pork and turkey. If you're feeling experimental, use that recipe as the base for your armadillo egg shell.

Chicken Armadillo Eggs

This version of delicious Armadillo Eggs uses seasoned ground chicken as the casing and a simple variation on traditional cream cheese filling. This version is also a bit lighter and lower in calories, like the ground turkey variation, though we've incorporated different seasonings.

Ingredients

- 10 jalapeno peppers
- 2 pounds ground chicken
- 1 egg, beaten
- 1/4 cup bread crumbs
- 10 ounces light cream cheese
- 1 teaspoon garlic, minced
- 1/2 teaspoon cumin
- 1/2 teaspoon ground coriander
- Salt and pepper to taste
- 2 cups chipotle mayonnaise (recipe below)

Cooking Directions

1. Remove stems from the jalapeno peppers and remove innards through the top with a pepper corer. If you do not have a corer, use a knife or very thin spoon.
2. In a mixing bowl, combine cream cheese, garlic, and salt and pepper to taste. Mix well.
3. Stuff about 1 ounce of your cheese mixture into each jalapeno pepper.
4. In a separate mixing bowl, combine ground chicken, cumin, coriander, egg and bread crumbs. Hand mix, but do not over mix.
5. Divide the ground chicken into 10 equal sizes patties and flatten with your hands. They should be just about 3 ounces each.
6. Mold one chicken patty around each jalapeno popper. Be sure to fully enclose the popper in the meat. Set onto a lightly oiled baking dish.
7. Preheat oven to 350 degrees.
8. Bake the Armadillo Eggs about 20-25 minutes, or until the meat is cooked through.
9. Serve with chipotle mayonnaise either over the top or on the side for dipping.

Chipotle Mayonnaise Recipe

We enjoy this simple yet delicious recipe on sandwiches but it goes great with Chicken Armadillo Eggs as a dipper.

Ingredients

- 2 cup mayonnaise
- 3-4 chipotle peppers in adobo sauce
- 1 teaspoon adobo sauce (from the can)
- 1 tablespoon fresh lime juice
- Salt to taste

Cooking Directions

1. To a food processor, add all ingredients and process until smooth.
2. Taste and adjust salt as needed.
3. Serve with your Chicken Armadillo Eggs!

Nacho Style Armadillo Eggs

This recipe is a combination of nacho flavors, with chorizo and spicy nacho cheese, though we've opted for ground chicken instead of ground beef. You can absolutely use ground beef instead of the chicken, though we enjoy both versions.

Ingredients

- 10 jalapeno peppers
- 2 pounds ground chicken
- 1 egg, beaten
- 1/4 cup bread crumbs
- 10 ounces cooked ground chorizo
- 2 cups easy nacho cheese (recipe below)

Cooking Directions

1. Remove stems from the jalapeno peppers and remove innards through the top with a pepper corer. If you do not have a corer, use a knife or very thin spoon.
2. Stuff about 1 ounce of chorizo into each jalapeno pepper.
3. In a mixing bowl, combine ground chicken, egg and bread crumbs. Hand mix, but do not over mix.
4. Divide the ground chicken into 10 equal sizes patties and flatten with your hands. They should be just about 3 ounces each.
5. Mold one chicken patty around each jalapeno popper. Be sure to fully enclose the popper in the meat. Set onto a lightly oiled baking dish.
6. Preheat oven to 350 degrees.
7. Bake the Armadillo Eggs about 20-25 minutes, or until the meat is cooked through.
8. Serve with nacho cheese either over the top or on the side for dipping.

Nacho Cheese Recipe

This cheese isn't just for serving over chips! Serve it over fries or anything else you prefer cheesy --- especially Armadillo Eggs!

Ingredients

- 8 slices processed American or Cheddar cheese, chopped
- 1 cup milk
- 2 tablespoons butter
- 2 tablespoons flour
- Salt to taste

Cooking Directions

1. Heat a saucepan to medium heat.
2. Add butter and melt. Stir in flour to form a roux. Cook about 3 minutes until flour mixture darkens.
3. Add milk and stir to thicken.
4. Add cheese slices in pieces, stirring constantly, until all the cheese is melted and uniform.
5. Salt to taste and serve with your Armadillo Eggs.

Stuffed Chili Peppers Recipes

Four-Cheese Stuffed Poblano Peppers

Poblano peppers are great for stuffing, as you can fit quite a lot of cheese inside, so consider the size of your poblano before preparation. We chose medium sized poblanos and were able to fit about 8 ounces of cheese inside, which will certainly fill you up.

Ingredients

- 2 medium sized Poblano peppers, stemmed and cored
- 2 ounces cream cheese
- 2 ounces shredded cheddar cheese
- 2 ounces crumbled feta cheese
- 2 ounces Parmesan cheese

Cooking Directions

1. In a mixing bowl combine all of your cheeses and mix well.
2. Stuff the poblano pepper with your cheese mixture.
3. Preheat grill to medium heat.
4. Wrap poblanos in aluminum foil and grill 12-15 minutes, or until done to your preference.
5. Serve.

Classic Chiles Rellenos

This traditional chiles rellenos recipe is a classic and also a must if you're a chili pepper lover. Translated, "chiles rellenos" is "stuffed chili peppers". While there are many, many variations for you to explore, you still can't go wrong with this classic, delicious recipe.

Ingredients

- 4 poblano peppers
- 2 eggs, separated
- ½ cup flour + ¼ cup, separated
- ½ cup milk
- 4 cheese slices (or equivalent of shredded cheese)
- Pinch of salt
- Pinch of baking powder
- Oil for frying

Cooking Directions

6. Roast the poblano peppers over an open flame, or use your oven broiler, until skins are blackened on each side. Over flame, it should only take about 5 minutes. In the broiler, it could take 10 or more minutes.
7. Remove poblano peppers and transfer to a plastic bag, and seal them up to let the skins loosen. Allow to cool.
8. Once cooled, peel off the blackened skins.
9. Slice open each poblano pepper lengthwise with one long slit, then remove the innards with a knife or spoon.
10. Stuff each pepper with cheese, but do not overstuff. Make sure you can still close the pepper.
11. Prepare your egg wash by beating the egg whites until stiff. Gently fold in the egg yolks and add to a bowl.
12. Prepare your batter in a separate bowl by combining ½ cup flour with ½ cup milk, pinch of baking powder and pinch of salt.

13. Pour oil into a pan, about 1 to 1-1/2 inches deep, in order to cover half the stuffed peppers when you drop them in.
14. In one more bowl, add the ¼ cup dry flour.
15. Dip each pepper into the dry flour to coat each side. Then, dip into the egg mixture, then into the batter to coat completely.
16. Fry each pepper about 2-3 minutes each side, or until they are a golden brown. The batter should sizzle up immediately after placing the peppers into the oil.
17. Drain excess oil and serve!

Random Tip

Chili Pepper Choices

So you want to make stuffed chili peppers but don't know which peppers to choose? Some peppers are better than others for stuffing. Your choice will depend on the meal occasion, serving size, heat level and more. If you're thinking appetizers, smaller peppers will work best for you, as they are bite sized, but beware. Some of the smaller peppers are hot! Larger peppers make for better main dishes.

Chiles Rellenos, Madness Style with Habanero-Mango Sauce

We love chiles rellenos so much that we created our own variation and served it up with our very own Habanero-Mango Sauce. The sweetness of the sauce plays beautifully with the Mexican-Parmesan cheese combination.

Ingredients

- FOR THE CHILES RELLENOS
- 4 poblano peppers
- 2 eggs, separated
- ½ cup flour + ¼ cup, separated
- ½ cup beer
- ½ cup Mexican cheese blend
- ½ cup Parmesan cheese
- Oil for frying
- FOR THE HABANERO-MANGO SAUCE
- 1 tablespoon olive oil
- ½ small onion, minced
- 1 teaspoon garlic, minced
- 1-2 habanero peppers
- 1 teaspoon fresh ginger, peeled and grated
- ½ teaspoon ground coriander
- 2 cups fresh mango, chopped
- 2 tablespoons apple cider vinegar
- ½ cup sugar
- Salt to taste
- Chili powder to taste

Cooking Directions

1. FOR THE HABANERO-MANGO SAUCE: Heat oil in a heavy saucepan to medium heat. Add onion, garlic, habanero, ginger and coriander. Cook 4 minutes to soften.
2. Add mango, sugar, chili powder, vinegar and salt to taste and cook, stirring, 8 minutes, or until the mango softens.
3. Transfer to a food processor and process until smooth.
4. Return to pan and cook over low heat, stirring frequently until thickened, about 15 minutes.
5. Cool and set aside until ready for use.
6. FOR THE CHILES RELLENOS: Roast the poblano peppers over an open flame, or use your oven broiler, until skins are blackened on each side. Over flame, it should only take about 5 minutes. In the broiler, it could take 10 or more minutes.
7. Remove poblano peppers and transfer to a plastic bag, and seal them up. Allow to cool.
8. Once cooled, peel off the blackened skins. Running them under water works great.
9. Slice open each poblano pepper lengthwise with one long slit, then remove the innards with a knife or spoon.
10. Stuff each pepper with cheese, but do not overstuff. Make sure you can still close the pepper.
11. Prepare your egg wash by beating the egg whites until stiff. Gently fold in the egg yolks and add to a bowl.
12. Prepare your batter in a separate bowl by combining ½ cup flour with ½ cup beer.
13. Pour oil into a pan, about 1 to 1-1/2 inches deep, in order to cover half the stuffed peppers when you drop them in.
14. In one more bowl, add the ¼ cup dry flour.
15. Dip each pepper into the dry flour to coat each side. Then, dip into the egg mixture, then into the batter to coat completely.
16. Fry each pepper about 2-3 minutes each side, or until they are a golden brown.
17. Drain excess oil and serve with the Habanero-Mango Sauce.

Turkey and Plum Stuffed Bell Peppers

This is not only a very tasty stuffed pepper dish, but it can also be extremely colorful if you choose either yellow or orange bell peppers. The color of the plum sauce plays against the brightness of the peppers. A dish like this is sure to impress your guests.

Ingredients

- FOR THE STUFFED PEPPERS
- 2 large orange bell peppers
- 12 ounces ground turkey
- 1 teaspoon chili powder
- 1 teaspoon tomato paste
- 1 teaspoon garlic, minced
- 2 cups spicy plum sauce (see ingredients below)
- Salt and pepper to taste
- 2 teaspoons olive oil
- FOR THE SPICY PLUM SAUCE
- 1 tablespoon olive oil
- ½ small onion, minced
- 1 teaspoon garlic, minced
- 1 jalapeno pepper, chopped (or habanero for heat!)
- 2 plums, pitted and chopped
- ¼ cup sugar
- ¼ cup water
- 1 teaspoon cornstarch dissolved in 1 tablespoon water
- 1-1/2 teaspoon soy sauce

Cooking Directions

1. FOR THE SPICY PLUM SAUCE: Heat oil in a heavy saucepan to medium heat. Add onion, garlic, jalapenos. Cook 5-6 minutes to soften.
2. Add plums, sugar and water and bring to a boil. Reduce heat to low and simmer until plums are soft, about 10 minutes.
3. Transfer to a food processor and process until smooth.
4. Return to pan and stir in cornstarch mixture.
5. Cook over low heat, stirring frequently until thickened, about 5 minutes
6. Stir in soy sauce and remove from heat. Allow to cool.
7. FOR THE STUFFED BELL PEPPERS: In a mixing bowl, combine turkey with tomato paste, chili powder, garlic, and salt and pepper to taste. Mix well.
8. Heat a large pan to medium heat and add olive oil. Add ground turkey mixture and cook about 10 minutes, or until turkey is cooked through.
9. Slice off the tops of the bell peppers and scoop out the insides. Keep the tops.
10. Stuff each pepper with 6 ounces of the turkey mixture, then top with 1 cup of your spicy plum sauce.
11. Preheat oven to 350 degrees.
12. Top the peppers and bake them on a lightly oiled baking sheet for 30-35 minutes, or until the peppers and nice and tender.
13. Serve!

Apple-Jalapeno Stuffed Poblano Peppers

Poblanos are perfect in so many ways. They're perfectly shaped for stuffing and have a delicious flavor, and they're also perfectly sized to make either a meal, side dish or appetizer. This stuffing combines the spicy jalapeno and the sweet apple for a delicious combination.

Ingredients

- 4 poblano peppers
- 2 jalapeno peppers, diced
- 1 apple, cored and diced
- 1/4 cup Parmesan cheese, shredded
- 4 ounces Italian sausage, cooked and crumbled
- 1 tablespoon Cajun seasonings
- 1/2 teaspoon cumin

Cooking Directions

1. Preheat oven to 350 degrees.
2. Cut tops off the poblano peppers and remove seeds.
3. In a large mixing bowl, combine apple, jalapeno peppers, Parmesan cheese, Italian sausage and seasonings. Mix well.
4. Stuff the mixture into your poblanos and place on a lightly spray-oiled baking sheet.
5. Bake 25-30 minutes, or until sausage is cooked thoroughly through.
6. Serve!

Cajun-Apple Stuffed Poblano Peppers

This recipe came to us after experimenting with various stuffing mixtures for pork chops. This one absolutely delivers on flavor. Chopped apples seasoned with Cajun spices make for a delicious stuffed poblano pepper. It's a perfect side dish. We also made a batch of Apple-Cajun Stuffed Jalapeno Peppers with the same mixture. So perfect!

Ingredients

- 2 large poblano peppers
- 1 apple, chopped
- 1 small onion, chopped
- 2 teaspoons Cajun seasonings
- 1 teaspoon dried chipotle flakes
- 2 tablespoons butter
- 1/4 cup bread crumbs
- Water as needed

Cooking Directions

1. Preheat oven to 350 degrees.
2. Slice poblano peppers in half lengthwise and remove seeds. Set aside.
3. Heat a frying pan to medium and add butter.
4. When butter is melted, stir in bread crumbs and mix well.
5. Add remaining ingredients and mix to combine. Use water in very small amounts to thin as needed, but the mixture should be slightly thick and chunky.
6. Fill each poblano half with a heaping mound of your stuffing mixture.
7. Bake stuffed poblanos on a lightly oiled baking sheet for 30 minutes.
8. Serve!

Cajun Cream Cheese Stuffed Anaheim Peppers

Anaheim peppers offer an alternative to grilled jalapeno poppers for those looking for less of a kick in the spice department. These are just as easy to make as jalapeno poppers.

Ingredients

- 10 Anaheim peppers, stemmed and cored
- 8 ounces cream cheese
- 2 ounces shredded cheddar cheese
- 2 tablespoons Cajun seasoning

Cooking Directions

1. In a mixing bowl, combine cheeses with Cajun seasoning.
2. Stuff Anaheims with 1 ounce of your cheese mixture.
3. Preheat grill to medium heat.
4. Wrap Anaheim peppers in aluminum foil and grill 10 minutes.
5. Serve.

Chorizo and Cheese Stuffed Poblano Peppers

Poblano peppers are the perfect size for stuffing. They go great as a side dish or as the focus of the main course, so be sure to plan accordingly. We coated ours in beer batter, though the batter isn't necessary. It's just plain good. NOTE: Your ingredients may vary depending on the size of the poblano peppers.

Ingredients

- 2 large poblano peppers
- 6 ounces chorizo, cooked
- 6 ounces shredded Mexican style cheese
- 4 ounces cream cheese
- 1 tablespoon chili powder
- 1 cup flour
- 1 cup beer

Cooking Directions

1. Preheat oven to 350 degrees.
2. Stem and core the poblano peppers, but retain the pepper tops.
3. In a mixing bowl, combine chorizo with cheeses and mix well. Stuff into poblano peppers.
4. Recap the peppers with the pepper tops. The cheese mixture should hold the tops in place.
5. In a separate mixing bowl, combine flour, beer and chili powder.
6. Dip stuffed poblano peppers into the beer batter, coating thoroughly.
7. Transfer to a lightly oiled pan and bake about 40 minutes, or until batter is golden brown.
8. Serve!

Italian Sausage and Cheese Stuffed Anaheim Peppers

Anaheim peppers are great for stuffing because, while they're long, they're also large enough to accommodate a good amount of stuffing. Also, for those with lower heat tolerances, the Anaheim pepper is not very spicy, with a Scoville Unit of 500-1000. You can easily spice it up if you want, but you can easily please the milder palate with this delicious pepper.

Ingredients

- 2 Anaheim peppers
- 1 Italian sausage link
- 2 ounces cheddar cheese (might need more)

Cooking Directions

1. Stem the peppers and remove the innards with a knife.
2. Heat a pan to medium heat and fry the Italian sausage. It helps to remove the sausage sheathe. Cook about 2 minutes, or until sausage is cooked through and crumbled. Allow to cool.
3. Stuff each pepper with layers of sausage and cheese. The amount will vary depending on the size of the pepper, so plan accordingly. Be sure to stuff the mixture in good and tight with your thumb.
4. Heat a grill to medium heat and grill for 15 minutes. It helps to wrap them in aluminum foil so the stuffing doesn't ooze out. If you grill directly over the heat, watch the skin for blackening, which is fine, but you don't want it TOO blackened.
5. Remove from heat and serve!

Fireballs

These flaming babies are great for a quick appetizer, but only if you've invited a group with a high heat tolerance. Even though the habanero peppers are cored, they still retain a healthy dose of heat. Enjoy!

Ingredients

- 20 small habanero peppers (or as many as you can stuff)
- 10 ounces cream cheese, softened
- 1 tablespoon chili powder

Cooking Directions

6. In a large mixing bowl, combine cream cheese and chili powder. Mix well.
7. Slice stems and about a quarter inch off the top of each habanero pepper. Scoop out the seeds with a spoon or tip of the knife.
8. Stuff each cored habanero with your spicy cream cheese mixture, about ½ ounce each. The amount may vary depending on the size of the habaneros.
9. Serve!

Sweet Fireballs

A sweeter variation of our spicy fireballs, these stuffed habanero peppers introduce jalapeno jelly for a different mood.

Ingredients

- 20 small habanero peppers (or as many as you can stuff)
- 8 ounces cream cheese, softened
- 4 ounces jalapeno pepper jelly

Cooking Directions

1. In a large mixing bowl, combine cream cheese and jalapeno pepper jelly. Mix well.
2. Slice stems and about a quarter inch off the top of each habanero pepper. Scoop out the seeds with a spoon or tip of the knife.
3. Stuff each cored habanero with your jelly-cream cheese mixture, about ½ ounce each. The amount may vary depending on the size of the habaneros.
4. Serve!

Ornery Goat Fireballs

Creamy goat cheese, almonds and fresh basil come together as a pesto-like stuffing. The creaminess of the goat cheese, however, gives it a different flavor and texture. Goat cheese teams nicely with almonds and basil. Stuffed into a spicy habanero and you have a simple appetizer with complex flavor.

Ingredients

- 20 small habanero peppers (or as many as you can stuff)
- 12-16 ounces goat cheese
- 4 ounces almonds, roasted and chopped
- 2-3 ounces fresh basil, chopped
- 1 teaspoon fresh garlic, minced

Cooking Directions

1. In a large mixing bowl, combine goat cheese, roasted almonds, garlic and basil. Mix well.
2. Slice stems and about a quarter inch off the top of each habanero pepper. Scoop out the seeds with a spoon or tip of the knife.
3. Stuff each cored habanero with your pesto-cheese mixture, about ½ ounce each. The amount may vary depending on the size of the habaneros.
4. Serve!

Fried Habanero Poppers

Get your inner popper "on" with these flaming habanero poppers. Definitely hotter than your traditional jalapeno poppers, these perfect little bite-sized portions will surely satisfy the heat lover in your life. Want to be even more daring? Try it with ghost peppers.

Ingredients

- 20 small habanero peppers (or as many as you can stuff)
- 6 ounces goat cheese
- 6 ounces cream cheese
- 1 teaspoon chili powder (hotter the better)
- 1 teaspoon chopped chives
- 2 eggs, separated
- ½ cup flour + ¼ cup, separated
- ½ cup milk
- Pinch of baking powder
- Pinch of salt
- Oil for frying

Cooking Directions

1. In a large mixing bowl, combine goat cheese, cream cheese, chili powder and chives. Mix well.
2. Slice stems and about a quarter inch off the top of each habanero pepper. Scoop out the seeds with a spoon or tip of the knife.
3. Stuff each cored habanero with your cheese mixture, about ½ ounce each. The amount may vary depending on the size of the habaneros.
4. Prepare your egg wash by beating the egg whites until stiff. Gently fold in the egg yolks and add to a bowl.
5. Prepare your batter in a separate bowl by combining ½ cup flour with ½ cup milk, pinch of baking powder and pinch of salt.

6. Pour oil into a pan, about 1 inch deep, in order to cover half the stuffed peppers when you drop them in. Heat oil to medium.
7. In one more bowl, add the ¼ cup dry flour.
8. Dip each pepper into the dry flour to coat each side. Then, dip into the egg mixture, then into the batter to coat completely.
9. Fry each pepper about 3-4 minutes each side, or until they are a golden brown. The batter should sizzle up immediately when you place the peppers into the oil.
10. Drain excess oil.
11. Serve!

Random Tip

Habanero Alternatives

Habanero peppers are wonderful, but be warned. They are quite hot. Habanero peppers rank at the higher end of the Scoville Heat Scale, up to 350,000 Scovilles. To compare, a jalapeno pepper is only 2,500 to 8,000 Scovilles. If you're looking for milder peppers of a similar size, try a milder Bishop's Crown or smaller aji peppers.

Pecan-Gouda Stuffed Cherry Bombs

If you can get yourself some good sized cherry bombs, snatch them up because they're perfect for small bite-sized appetizers or for side dishes. Here, we've paired Gouda cheese with roasted pecans and a touch of garlic to even things out. What a combination!

Ingredients

- 20 cherry bomb peppers (or as many as you can stuff)
- 20 ounces Gouda cheese, shredded
- 4 ounces pecans, roasted and chopped
- 1 teaspoon fresh garlic, minced
- Salt to taste

Cooking Directions

1. Preheat oven to 350 degrees.
2. In a large mixing bowl, combine Gouda cheese, roasted pecans, garlic and salt to taste. Mix well.
3. Slice stems and about a quarter inch off the top of each cherry bomb pepper. Scoop out the seeds with a spoon or tip of the knife.
4. Stuff each cored pepper with your cheese stuffing mixture, about 1 ounce each. The amount may vary depending on the size of the peppers.
5. Bake stuffed peppers on a baking dish for 20-25 minutes.
6. Allow to cool slightly and serve!

NOTE: These can be served cold, without baking, as well, though we prefer them warmed. The cheese melts evenly and the peppers are softer, though they're great uncooked as well.

Bada Bing Bombs

If you can get yourself some good sized cherry bombs, snatch them up because they're perfect for small bite-sized appetizers or for side dishes. For the Bada Bing Bombs, we've introduced one of the tastiest deli meats around – pepperoni! It has such a distinctive flavor. Vary up the ratio of pepperoni to cream cheese and see how you like the results.

Ingredients

- 20 cherry bomb peppers (or as many as you can stuff)
- 20 ounces cream cheese, softened
- 4 ounces pepperoni slices, chopped
- 1 teaspoon fresh garlic, minced
- 1 teaspoon chili powder
- Salt to taste

Cooking Directions

1. Preheat oven to 350 degrees.
2. In a large mixing bowl, combine cream cheese, pepperoni, chili powder, garlic and salt to taste. Mix well.
3. Slice stems and about a quarter inch off the top of each cherry bomb pepper. Scoop out the seeds with a spoon or tip of the knife.
4. Stuff each cored pepper with your pepperoni-cheese stuffing mixture, about 1 ounce each. The amount may vary depending on the size of the peppers.
5. Bake stuffed peppers on a baking dish for 20 minutes.
6. Allow to cool slightly and serve!

Turkey Meatball-Stuffed Cubanelles with Jalapeno-Strawberry BBQ Sauce

The Cubanelle is considered a sweet pepper, although its heat can range from mild to moderate. Cubanelles are usually picked before they ripen, while they are a yellowish-green color, but when ripe, they turn bright red. Since it is full of flavor but not very hot, we paired it with a spicy barbecue sauce with strawberries to compliment the sweetness.

Ingredients

- FOR THE STUFFED PEPPERS
- 4-6 large Cubanelle peppers
- 1 pound ground turkey
- ¼ cup Romano cheese, shredded
- ¼ cup bread crumbs
- 2 teaspoons tomato paste
- 1 teaspoon garlic, minced
- Salt and pepper to taste
- 2 teaspoons olive oil
- FOR THE JALAPENO-STRAWBERRY BBQ SAUCE
- 6-8 strawberries, stemmed and chopped
- 4 jalapeno peppers, chopped
- 1 tablespoon tomato paste
- ½ onion, chopped
- 1 garlic clove, minced
- ¼ cup sugar
- 2 tablespoons apple cider vinegar
- 2 tablespoons fresh lemon juice
- 1 teaspoon chili powder
- ½ teaspoon ground ginger
- Salt to taste

Cooking Directions

1. FOR THE JALAPENO-STRAWBERRY BBQ SAUCE: To a food processor or blender, add strawberries, jalapenos, tomato paste, onion, garlic, sugar, vinegar, lemon juice, chili powder and ginger. Process until smooth.
2. Heat a saucepan to medium-low heat.
3. Strain the Jalapeno-Strawberry mixture into the pan and simmer about 15 minutes to thicken.
4. Salt to taste and reserve.
5. FOR THE STUFFED CUBANELLE PEPPERS: In a mixing bowl, combine turkey with tomato paste, bread crumbs, cheese, garlic, and salt and pepper to taste. Mix well.
6. Form the turkey mixture into small meatballs, about 1 ounce or less in size. You should wind up with 16-20 meatballs.
7. Heat a large pan to medium heat and add olive oil. Add meatballs and cook about 10 minutes, or until turkey is cooked mostly through.
8. Slice the Cubanelle peppers in half lengthwise and remove the innards.
9. Add 3-4 meatballs to each pepper half.
10. Preheat oven to 350 degrees.
11. Bake the Cubanelle peppers on a lightly oiled baking sheet for 20 minutes, or until the peppers and nice and tender.
12. Top with Jalapeno-Strawberry BBQ Sauce and serve!

Sweet Peppers Stuffed with Flaming Potato Pesto

Sweet Peppers like the large ancient sweet make for great stuffing peppers. They have a great flavor and they're large enough to accommodate a good amount of stuffing, which goes well for a hearty meal. We love our food to be spicy, and since the peppers are sweet and not very hot, we decided to heat it up with the stuffing.

Ingredients

- 2 large ancient sweet peppers
- 1 pound potatoes, peeled and chopped
- 1 teaspoon minced garlic
- 10 fresh basil leaves, coarsely chopped
- ¼ cup almonds, coarsely chopped
- 2 tablespoons olive oil
- Additional oil for cooking
- Chili powder or paprika to taste

Cooking Directions

1. Heat a pan to medium heat and lightly coat with oil.
2. Add the potatoes and cook about 5 minutes. Or until they begin to soften.
3. Add chopped almonds and cook an additional 5 minutes. Do not allow almonds to burn.
4. Transfer potatoes and almonds to a food processor or blender. Add garlic, basil leaves and 2 tablespoons olive oil. Pulse a few times to keep pesto nice and chunky.
5. Slice the sweet peppers in half lengthwise and remove the insides.
6. Divide the pesto mixture between the 4 pepper slices.
7. Preheat oven to 350 degrees.
8. Place peppers on a lightly oiled baking sheet and bake for 20 minutes.
9. Dust with chili powder or paprika and serve!

Strawberry-Banana Pepper Poppers

Why stuff a pepper with a strawberry when you can stuff a strawberry with a pepper! These cute little poppers are great for a quick appetizer since they're so easy to make, but they also make for a unique dessert.

Ingredients

- 10 strawberries
- 5 ounces cream cheese, softened
- 1 banana pepper, chopped
- 1 teaspoon sugar
- 1 teaspoon chili powder

Cooking Directions

1. Slice off the top of each strawberry and a tiny portion of the bottom to flatten it so they can stand up on their own.
2. Scoop out most of the insides of the strawberries with a knife or small spoon. Be sure to keep the integrity of the strawberry walls, and don't dig too far in through the bottom.
3. In a mixing bowl, combine cream cheese, banana pepper slices, sugar and chili powder. Mix well.
4. Stuff each strawberry with about ½ ounce each of the cream cheese mixture.
5. Serve!

Taco Stuffed
Cherry Peppers

Cherry peppers have a nice little kick, but aren't too spicy. They are also perfectly shaped for stuffing and perfectly sized for appetizers, so these can be a popular choice for your next party. A single stuffed cherry pepper can be finished in just a couple of bites.

Ingredients

- 1 small avocado
- 2 ounces cream cheese, softened
- 2 tablespoons fresh cilantro, chopped
- Pinch salt
- 1 tablespoon fresh squeezed orange juice
- 1 teaspoon fresh squeezed lemon juice
- ½ teaspoon fresh lemon zest
- 1 teaspoon taco seasoning or chili powder
- 6 cherry peppers

Cooking Directions

1. Slice the tops off the cherry peppers and set aside. Core the peppers, ensuring not to pierce the outer skin.
2. In a mixing bowl, combine the remaining ingredients. Mix well.
3. Spoon your mixture into the hollowed out cherry peppers.
4. Top with your sliced-off tops and serve!

Goat Cheese and Romano Stuffed Poblanos

This recipe is on the milder side of spicy, but is filled with strong flavor blasts from the combination of goat cheese and the Romano cheese. The roasted almonds and basil bring a bit of a pesto flair, but the cheese here is the true focus - perfect for poblano peppers.

Ingredients

- 2 large poblano peppers
- 3 ounces goat cheese
- 5 ounces Romano cheese, grated
- 2 ounces almonds
- 8 large basil leaves, chopped
- Olive oil

Cooking Directions

1. Preheat oven to 350 degrees.
2. Remove stems and seeds from poblano peppers. Slice them in half lengthwise and set them into a lightly oiled baking dish.
3. Heat a sauté pan to medium heat and add almonds with a splash of olive oil. Roast about 5 minutes, or until nuts begin to brown.
4. Transfer almonds to a food processor with basil leaves. Process until chunky. Allow to cool.
5. Transfer almond-basil mixture to a mixing bowl with goat cheese and Romano cheese. Mix well.
6. Heap your stuffing mixture into each poblano pepper half. Distribute evenly.
7. Bake 25-35 minutes, or until poblanos are softened.
8. Serve!

Stuffed Pepper Soup

Get all the flavors of your favorite stuffed pepper recipes in a bowl of soup. It's a warm and hearty variation filled with flavor, perfect on a cold winter day. This recipe makes 4 bowls.

Ingredients

- 1/2 pound ground turkey
- 1 green bell pepper, chopped
- 1 yellow bell pepper, chopped
- 1 small onion, chopped
- 1 clove fresh garlic, minced
- 1 (15 ounces) can diced tomatoes
- 1 (15 ounces) can tomato sauce
- 1 tablespoon tomato paste
- 16 ounces vegetable stock
- 1/4 teaspoon dried thyme
- 1/4 teaspoon dried basil
- salt and pepper to taste
- Cayenne pepper to taste
- 1/3 cup white rice; uncooked
- 1 tablespoon olive oil

Cooking Directions

1. Heat a large pan to medium heat and add ground turkey with 2 tablespoons water. Cook about 10 minutes, or until cooked through. Break apart and set aside.
2. To the pan, add bell peppers and onion with olive oil. Cook about 5 minutes, or until vegetables are softened.
3. Add garlic and cook 1 more minute.
4. Add diced tomatoes, tomato sauce, tomato paste, vegetable stock, thyme and basil. Season to taste with salt, pepper, and cayenne pepper.
5. Stir in white rice and cooked turkey.
6. Cover and simmer over low heat for 25 to 30 minutes, until rice is cooked through.
7. Serve with crusty bread.

NOTE: You can vary the thickness levels of this soup by adding more vegetable stock or water to thin it out, or adding more rice for a thicker soup.

Mexican Style Stuffed Peppers

Get a burst of delicious Mexican-style flavors in these stuffed red bell peppers. As a colorful variation, serve red, green and yellow stuffed bell peppers with the same ingredients. The presentation will look very inviting. Choose a ground beef that isn't so lean for a fuller flavor.

Ingredients

- 1 pound ground beef
- 6 red bell peppers
- 1 small yellow onion, chopped
- 1 stalk celery, chopped
- 1 clove garlic, minced
- 3 cups brown rice, cooked
- 2 cups salsa
- 4 tablespoons chili powder
- 1 cup Mexican style cheese
- Chopped cilantro to garnish

Cooking Directions

1. Remove the stems and seeds from the bell peppers.
2. Bring a large pot of water to boil and boil the hollowed peppers for 4 minutes. Drain and set aside.
3. Heat a large pan to medium heat. Add ground beef and cook about 5 minutes, until meat begins to brown.
4. Add onion and celery and cook another 5 minutes.
5. Add garlic and stir. Cook about 1 more minute, or until the beef is cooked through.
6. Stir in the brown rice, salsa and chili powder. Mix well.
7. Fill the peppers with your meat mixture and set onto a baking dish.
8. Preheat oven to 350 degrees and bake about 35 minutes, or until peppers are heated through.
9. Sprinkle cheese over the pepper tops and bake another 3 minutes to melt the cheese.
10. Garnish with chopped cilantro and serve!

Veal and Risotto Stuffed Peppers

This stuffed pepper recipe has a strong Italian focus with the veal and risotto, which is nice and creamy and best when cooked slowly, allowing the creaminess and flavors to develop. Stuff it all into a pepper and you're in heaven. This is a traditional method for preparing a risotto, with some Italian seasonings and tomato sauce added.

Ingredients

- 6 red bell peppers
- 1 bunch scallions, chopped
- 1 large carrot, chopped
- 3 cloves of garlic, chopped
- 2 tablespoons olive oil
- 1 pound of ground veal
- 1 cup of Arborio rice
- 1/2 cup white wine
- 1 teaspoon dried tarragon
- 1 teaspoon thyme
- 6 cups chicken broth
- 8 ounces tomato sauce
- 8 ounces Romano cheese, shredded
- 1 teaspoon salt
- 1 teaspoon fresh ground black pepper
- 2 tablespoons dried parsley
- 12 ounces mozzarella cheese, shredded
- 16 ounces tomato sauce
- 2 tablespoons dried basil

Cooking Directions

1. Remove the stems and seeds from the bell peppers.
2. Bring a large pot of water to boil and boil the hollowed peppers for 4 minutes to soften. Drain and set aside.
3. Heat a large pan to medium heat and add carrot and scallions with 2 tablespoons olive oil. Cook 5 minutes, or until vegetables begin to soften.
4. Add garlic and cook another minute.
5. Add ground veal and break apart. Cook about 5 minutes, or until veal begins to brown.
6. Add Arborio rice and cook about 3 minutes, stirring often, until rice is browned.
7. Add white wine and stir until wine is absorbed into the rice, about 2-3 minutes.
8. Stir in tarragon and thyme.
9. Add chicken broth one cup at a time and stir frequently. Once broth is absorbed, about 8-10 minutes or so, add another cup of broth and continue, until all the broth is absorbed.
10. Stir in 8 ounces tomato sauce, shredded Romano cheese, parsley, salt and pepper. Stir until cheese is melted and all ingredients are combined.
11. Stuff each bell pepper with your veal-risotto mixture and place them on a deep baking dish. Top each with 2 ounces freshly shredded mozzarella cheese.
12. Fill baking dish with 16 ounces tomato sauce. Season with dried basil flakes.
13. Bake at 350 degrees about 20 minutes, or until cheese is nice and melted.
14. Serve!

Chili Con Queso
Stuffed Cubanelle Peppers

Chili con Queso is a very popular as a dipper side dish, typically served with chips. Our version works great stuffed into a Cubanelle pepper, which is a tad bit spicier than a bell, though still quite mild in general. Most of the heat from this recipe will come from your choice of chili peppers added to the Chili con Queso itself, so feel free to make it as hot as you'd like.

Ingredients

- 4 small chili peppers, diced
  (try jalapenos for medium heat, cayenne peppers for some extra blast, or habaneros for the real fire)
- 1 ten-ounce can diced tomatoes
- 2 teaspoons olive oil
- 1 small onion, chopped
- 2 cloves garlic, minced
- 1/2 cup pale ale
- 1 plus 1/2 cups low-fat milk, divided
- 3 tablespoons cornstarch
- 1 3/4 cups shredded sharp Cheddar, preferably orange
- 2 tablespoons lime juice
- 1 teaspoon salt
- 1 teaspoon chili powder
- 1 teaspoon cayenne pepper, to taste
- 10 Cubanelle Chili Peppers

Cooking Directions

1. Heat oil in a large saucepan over medium heat.
2. Add onion and garlic and cook, stirring, until soft, 4 to 5 minutes.
3. Add beer and cook until reduced slightly, about 1 minute.
4. Add 1 cup milk and simmer.

5. Meanwhile, whisk remaining 1/2 cup milk and cornstarch in a small bowl. Add to pan and cook, stirring vigorously, until bubbling and thickened, 1 to 2 minutes.
6. Reduce heat to low, add cheese and cook, stirring, until melted.
7. Stir in drained tomatoes, lime juice, salt, chili powder and cayenne.
8. Keep warm.
9. Remove stems from Cubanelle peppers, then slice in half lengthwise and remove the seeds and innards.
10. Preheat oven to 350 degrees.
11. Bring a large pot of water to boil and boil the peppers about 4 minutes to soften. Remove and set onto a large baking dish.
12. Spoon the chili con queso into the Cubanelle peppers and bake 20 minutes, or until peppers are nice and soft.
13. Serve!

Random Tip

Chili Pepper Color

Consider the color of your pepper before you embark on your stuffed chili pepper meal if you'd like to make a pleasant presentation.
Chili pepper colors will vary from pepper to pepper and range from bright green to dark green to various shades of orange, yellow or red.
While taste is of utmost importance to your meal, your presentation and color choices can help make your stuffed peppers more inviting.

Sweet Stuffed Bell Peppers

This stuffed pepper recipe is a variation of the traditional seasoned beef and rice stuffed peppers, but with honey as a sweetener along with developed Cajun and chili pepper seasonings. We typically opt for a habanero powder seasoning from our own dried peppers we produce each year, but any chili powder will do for flavor.

Ingredients

- 4 large green or red bell peppers
- 1 pound ground beef
- 1 medium white onion, diced
- 2 1/2 cups cooked Jasmine white rice, set aside
- 2 garlic cloves, minced
- 1 teaspoon Cajun seasonings
- 1 teaspoon chili pepper seasoning
- 2 15 ounce cans tomato sauce
- 8 tablespoons honey

Cooking Directions

1. In a large frying pan, add onion and ground beef. Sauté until beef is browned, about 5 minutes.
2. Drain fat and add prepared rice, garlic, and seasonings. Mix well.
3. Slice bell peppers in half. Remove caps and seeds.
4. In a mixing bowl, combine 1 can of tomato sauce and 4 tablespoons honey. Mix well.
5. Add tomato sauce to frying pan with beef and rice.
6. In same mixing bowl, combine remaining tomato sauce and honey. Set aside.
7. Spoon the beef and rice mixture into bell pepper halves.
8. Arrange stuffed bell peppers over a lightly oiled baking dish.
9. Pour reserved tomato-honey sauce over the stuffed peppers and bake 1 hour at 325 degrees.
10. Cool and serve!

Slow Cooker Stuffed Peppers

Most of our recipes call for baking the stuffed peppers, as it is more traditional and very simple, but slow cooking your peppers is just as easy. Cook your stuffed peppers over very low heat for a long time, about 4 hours, and you'll enjoy a wonderful meal when it comes time for dinner. This version is extra spicy with the habanero peppers, but feel free to substitute them for something milder to your tastes.

Ingredients

- 4 large bell peppers
- 2 habanero peppers, chopped
- 1 pound ground turkey
- 1/2 cup quinoa, uncooked
- 1/4 cup chopped cilantro
- 1 small onion, chopped
- 1 clove garlic, minced
- 2 cups vegetable broth
- 1 can (28 ounces) tomato sauce
- 1 tablespoon dried basil
- 1 tablespoon dried oregano
- Salt and pepper to taste

Cooking Directions

1. In a large bowl, combine ground turkey, quinoa, habanero peppers, cilantro, onion and garlic. Break up turkey and mix well.
2. Remove the stems, seeds and innards from the bell peppers.
3. Divide the turkey mixture and stuff into each pepper.
4. Set the peppers into a slow cooker on low.
5. In a separate mixing bowl, combine vegetable broth, tomato sauce, basil, oregano and salt and pepper. Mix well.
6. Pour sauce over the peppers and cover.
7. Cook on medium about 4 hours. Alternatively, you can cook for several hours longer on low heat.
8. Serve!

Egg Salad
Stuffed Paprika Peppers

The paprika is a fairly large red pepper and quite long, growing up to 8 inches, and lends a unique spiciness to paprika powder. They are typically dried and ground to make the more familiar powdered spice. They more commonly added to dishes for color, but lend themselves perfectly to stuffed pepper recipes. Here is a version with egg salad.

Ingredients

- 6 paprika peppers
- 5 large eggs
- 2 tablespoons mayonnaise
- 1 tablespoon spicy brown mustard
- 1 small avocado, peeled and pitted
- Salt to taste

Cooking Directions

1. Preheat oven to 350 degrees.
2. Remove stems from the paprika peppers and slice in half lengthwise. Remove the pepper innards.
3. Set peppers onto a large baking sheet, skin sides up, and bake about 20 minutes, or until skins are blackened. Remove from heat and add to a bowl. Cover to allow peppers to steam. This will loosen the skins.
4. Once peppers are cooled, peel off skins and set onto a serving dish.
5. Heat a small pot of water to boil and add eggs. Boil for 12 minutes, until eggs are hard boiled. Remove from heat, cool slightly and peel. Add eggs to a large mixing bowl.
6. To mixing bowl, add mayonnaise, mustard, avocado and salt. Mix well, ensuring the avocado and eggs are nicely mashed yet still chunky.
7. Spoon mixture over roasted peppers and serve.

Potato Salad
Stuffed Paprika Peppers

The paprika is a fairly large red pepper and quite long, growing up to 8 inches, and lends a unique spiciness to paprika powder. They are typically dried and ground to make the more familiar powdered spice. They more commonly added to dishes for color, but lend themselves perfectly to stuffed pepper recipes. Here is a version with potato salad.

Ingredients

- 6 paprika peppers
- 12 small red potatoes
- 2 tablespoons pickle juice (great if you can get it from pickled jalapenos)
- 2 tablespoons celery, finely chopped
- 2 tablespoons mayonnaise
- 1 tablespoon spicy brown mustard
- 1/4 cup chopped parsley
- Salt to taste

Cooking Directions

1. Preheat oven to 350 degrees.
2. Remove stems from the paprika peppers and slice in half lengthwise. Remove the pepper innards.
3. Set peppers onto a large baking sheet, skin sides up, and bake about 20 minutes, or until skins are blackened. Remove from heat and add to a bowl. Cover to allow peppers to steam. This will loosen the skins.
4. Once peppers are cooled, peel off skins and set onto a serving dish.
5. Heat a small pot of water to boil and add potatoes. Boil for 20 minutes, until potatoes are softened. Remove from heat, drain, and add to a large mixing bowl.
6. To mixing bowl, add mayonnaise, mustard, pickle juice, celery, parsley and salt. Mix well.
7. Spoon mixture over roasted peppers and serve.

Jamaican Jerk Chicken Stuffed Paprika Peppers

The paprika is a fairly large red pepper and quite long, growing up to 8 inches, and lends a unique spiciness to paprika powder. They are typically dried and ground to make the more familiar powdered spice. They are more commonly added to dishes for color, but lend themselves perfectly to stuffed pepper recipes. Here is a version with spicy Jamaican Jerk Chicken. It is quite spicy with the scotch bonnet chili pepper.

Ingredients

- 6 paprika peppers
- 2 chicken breasts
- 1 Scotch Bonnet pepper, chopped
- 1 cayenne pepper, chopped
- 2 tablespoons olive oil
- 2 tablespoons soy sauce
- 1/4 cup white vinegar
- 1/4 cup orange juice
- 1 teaspoon lime juice
- 2 green onions, chopped
- 1 small white onion, chopped
- 1 teaspoon ground sage
- 1/4 teaspoon nutmeg
- 1/4 teaspoon cinnamon
- 1 teaspoon allspice, ground
- 1 teaspoon dried thyme
- 1/2 teaspoon pepper
- 1 tablespoons garlic, minced
- 1 teaspoon sugar
- Salt to taste

Cooking Directions

1. In a mixing bowl, combine the allspice, thyme, cayenne pepper, black pepper, sage, nutmeg, cinnamon, salt, garlic and sugar.
2. Add olive oil, soy sauce, vinegar, orange juice, and lime juice. Mix well.
3. Add scotch bonnet peppers and onions. Combine.
4. Add chicken and toss to coat. Cover and marinate 2-4 hours.
5. Preheat oven to 350 degrees.
6. Remove stems from the paprika peppers and slice in half lengthwise. Remove the pepper innards.
7. Set peppers onto a large baking sheet, skin sides up, and bake about 20 minutes, or until skins are blackened. Remove from heat and add to a bowl. Cover to allow peppers to steam. This will loosen the skins.
8. Once peppers are cooled, peel off skins and set onto a serving dish.
9. Preheat a large sauté pan or grill to medium heat.
10. Remove chicken from marinade and sauté 5-6 minutes per side, or until thoroughly cooked through and no longer pink in the center. Discard the marinade.
11. Chop chicken into small cubes and spoon mixture over roasted peppers.
12. Serve!

NOTE: As a variation, you can sprinkle some white cheese over the tops of the chicken and bake about 5 minutes to melt the cheese. Or, serve with a bit of Mango-Scotch Bonnet Sauce. We have the recipe for that online at www.chilipeppermadness.com.

Shrimp Scampi Stuffed Peppers

This recipe is a version of a scampi recipe we created with a spicy habanero focus. Try sweet bell peppers, poblanos, or larger Cubanelle peppers with this recipe.

Ingredients

- 4 medium to large chili peppers
- 1 pound large shrimp or prawns, coarsely chopped
- 2 habanero peppers, chopped
- 1 stick butter
- 8 garlic cloves, finely diced
- 4 teaspoons white cooking wine
- 4 tablespoons lemon juice
- 1 teaspoon lemon zest
- 1 teaspoon red pepper flakes
- 1 tablespoon chili powder
- Salt and pepper to taste
- 1 tablespoon fresh parsley, chopped
- 1 teaspoon olive oil
- 1/2 cup bread crumbs

Cooking Directions

1. Remove the stems from the peppers and slice them in half lengthwise.
2. Remove seeds and innards and discard.
3. Bring a large pot of water to boil and boil the peppers for 4 minutes to soften. Drain and set aside.
4. Add shrimp to a mixing bowl and season with chili powder, red pepper flakes, salt and pepper.
5. Heat a sauté pan to medium heat. Add olive oil, garlic, and habanero peppers.
6. Sauté about 1 minute and then add butter and melt down. Stir.

7. Add shrimp and simmer 3-4 minutes or until shrimp is thoroughly cooked through.

8. Add white wine, lemon juice, lemon zest and parsley and stir. Remove from heat.

9. Stir in bread crumbs and mix to thicken.

10. Set peppers onto a baking dish and fill each with equal amounts of the scampi mixture.

11. Bake at 350 degrees for 20 minutes.

12. Remove from heat and allow to cool slightly before serving.

NOTE: If you'd like your scampi mixture to be thicker, you can add more bread crumbs as needed.

Random Tip

Get Your Grill On

Grilling is a great alternative to baking for stuffed peppers.
If you're like us, you love to cook outside when the weather is
nice and warm. If you decide to grill, aluminum foil will make your
job easier. Wrap your peppers in foil then place them on the medium-heat
grill, avoiding direct flame. The foil will seal in the heat and also
keep your stuffing intact.

White Bean, Pumpkin and Cheese Stuffed Peppers

This recipe is a tasty variation on a holiday pumpkin-bean dip recipe, which brings the flavors into poblano peppers.

Ingredients

- 6-8 large poblano peppers
- 2 jalapeno peppers
- 1 cup canned pumpkin
- 1 (15 ounce) can of white northern beans, drained
- 8 ounces cream cheese, softened
- 4 ounces freshly grated Romano cheese
- 2 tablespoons olive oil
- 2 tablespoons lemon juice
- 4 cloves fresh garlic
- Salt to taste
- Bread crumbs for topping

Cooking Directions

1. Remove the stems from the jalapeno peppers and slice them in half lengthwise.
2. Place the jalapenos on a baking sheet, skin sides up. Add garlic cloves.
3. Broil in a preheated oven about 15 minutes, or until the jalapeno pepper skins blacken and char.
4. Remove blackened skin, if desired, and chop the jalapeno peppers. Add to a food processor.
5. Squeeze the garlic from the skins into the food processor.
6. Add remaining ingredients to food processor and process until creamy. NOTE: You can always add more olive oil to achieve a creamier texture. Just stream the oil into the mixture while processing on low until your desired texture is reached.

7. Cut off the stems of the poblano peppers and slice in half lengthwise. Remove seeds and pepper innards.
8. Preheat oven to 350 degrees.
9. Set poblano peppers skin side down on a lightly oiled baking dish and spoon pumpkin-bean mixture into the poblanos.
10. Sprinkle bread crumbs over the tops of the filled poblano peppers and bake for 20-30 minutes, or until peppers are softened and bread crumbs are browned.
11. Serve!

Chicken Satay Stuffed Peppers

There is a delicious richness to this peanut sauce that truly lends itself to a stuffed pepper. Yellow bell peppers are great for color for this recipe, but any bell or large pepper will serve you. Also, we used chicken tenders here, but chicken breast is fine as well.

Ingredients

- FOR THE PEPPERS
- 6 large yellow bell peppers
- 2 pounds chicken tenders
- 1 teaspoon olive oil
- 2 tablespoons white wine
- FOR THE MARINADE
- 1 small onion, chopped
- 1 teaspoon olive oil
- 1 teaspoon fresh garlic, minced
- 2 habanero peppers, chopped
- 1 poblano pepper, roasted, stemmed and seeded
- 1/2 teaspoon ground ginger
- 1/2 teaspoon turmeric
- 1/4 cup soy sauce
- 1 tablespoon brown sugar
- Salt and pepper to taste
- FOR THE PEANUT SAUCE
- 1 small onion, chopped
- 1 teaspoon olive oil
- 2-3 teaspoons red curry paste
- 1/2 cup water
- 1 tablespoon sugar
- 1/2 cup peanut butter
- 2 tablespoons lime juice
- Salt to taste

Cooking Directions

1. MARINADE: Sauté onion in olive oil about 5 minutes over medium heat.
2. Add minced garlic and cook 1 minute. Stir and remove from heat. Add to a mixing bowl.
3. To the bowl, add roasted poblano pepper, habanero peppers, ground ginger, turmeric, soy sauce, and brown sugar. Add salt and pepper to taste. Stir.
4. Add your chicken strips to the marinade and stir to coat.
5. Cover the bowl or transfer contents to a baggie and seal. Refrigerate about 4 hours, or overnight for more flavor.
6. CHICKEN: Heat a sauté pan to medium-high heat. Coarsely chop the chicken and sear the pieces about 1 minute each side, then reduce heat to medium.
7. Add white wine to deglaze chicken, and cook about 5-6 more minutes, or until chicken is cooked through. Set chicken aside.
8. PEANUT SAUCE: In a large pan, sauté onion in olive oil about 5 minutes over medium heat.
9. Add 2-3 teaspoons red curry paste and stir. Cook about 2 minutes.
10. Add 1/2 cup water and 1 tablespoon sugar. Bring to a boil and stir.
11. Add 1/2 cup peanut butter and whisk it together.
12. Reduce heat and simmer about 5 minutes.
13. Add more water at this point to achieve your desired consistency.
14. Add chicken into the sauce and cook about 5 minutes, or until chicken is warmed.
15. Remove from heat, then stir in lime juice and salt to taste. Set aside.
16. STUFFED PEPPERS: Cut off the tops of the peppers and scoop out the insides of the pepper. Rinse.
17. Bring a large pot of water to boil. Boil the peppers about 4 minutes each to soften.
18. Preheat oven to 350 degrees.
19. Set peppers onto a baking dish and divide chicken satay mixture between them, filling each pepper.
20. Bake the peppers 20-30 minutes or until peppers are softened.
21. Serve!

Chicken Stuffed Peppers with Chipotle-Bacon-Bourbon Barbecue Sauce

The combination of chipotle and barbecue sauce is a double flavor whammy for chicken. Stuff them into peppers and you now have yourself a triple flavor threat. Great stuff.

Ingredients

- FOR THE PEPPERS
- 2 large red bell peppers
- 1 large chicken breast
- 1 tablespoon olive oil
- FOR THE CHIPOTLE-BACON-BOURBON BARBECUE SAUCE
- 2 7-ounce cans chipotle peppers in adobo
- 8 ounces bacon, chopped
- 2 cups ketchup
- 1 cup cider vinegar
- 1 cup light brown sugar
- 12 tablespoons Worcestershire sauce
- 8 tablespoons Jim Beam bourbon
- 4 tablespoons molasses
- 4 teaspoons ground chili guajillo
- 2 small yellow onions, chopped
- 4 teaspoons fresh minced garlic
- 4 teaspoons paprika
- 2 teaspoon ground mustard seeds
- Salt and pepper to taste

Cooking Directions

1. FOR THE CHICKEN: Heat a grill to medium heat.
2. Season chicken breast with salt and pepper and slice it into thin pieces.
3. Brush chicken slices with olive oil and grill them about 8-10 minutes, flipping once half way through, or until chicken is cooked through.
4. Remove from heat and chop. Set aside.
5. FOR THE SAUCE: Heat a large saucepan to medium heat and add bacon. Cook about 5 minutes, stirring often.
6. Add onion and cook 3 more minutes, stirring often, until bacon is nice and crisp.
7. Add garlic and cook 1 more minute, or until garlic browns nicely.
8. Add remaining ingredients and mix well.
9. Bring sauce to a boil and reduce heat to low. Simmer 30 minutes with an occasional stir. The sauce will slightly thicken.
10. PEPPERS: Prepare your peppers by cutting off the top portion and scooping out the insides. Rinse.
11. Bring a large pot of water to boil. Boil the peppers about 4 minutes each to soften.
12. Preheat oven to 350 degrees.
13. Place peppers onto a lightly oiled deep baking dish. Stuff peppers with chopped chicken.
14. Partially fill with your barbecue sauce, then pour remaining sauce into baking dish around the peppers.
15. Bake 20-30 minutes, or until the peppers have softened.
16. Serve!

Hawaiian Chicken Stuffed Peppers with Pineapple Relish

Get the grill ready for this sweet pineapple marinated chicken stuffed into delicious peppers and served with pineapple relish. Go, pineapple! A great meal before catching some waves...or being lazy on the beach.

Ingredients

- 4 red bell peppers or large sweet peppers
- 2 chicken breasts
- ¼ cup soy sauce
- ¼ cup pineapple juice
- ¼ cup olive oil
- ¼ cup brown sugar
- 1 teaspoon ginger powder
- ½ teaspoon salt
- 1 teaspoon cayenne powder
- FOR THE PINEAPPLE RELISH
- 2 jalapeno peppers, diced
- Fruit from one pineapple, chopped (or use one 14 ounce can pineapple slices in juice)
- 2 tablespoons brown sugar
- 2 tablespoons wine vinegar
- 1 teaspoon garlic, minced
- 2 scallions, chopped
- ¼ cup fresh cilantro, coarsely chopped
- Salt and pepper to taste

Cooking Directions

1. FOR THE CHICKEN: In a mixing bowl, combine soy sauce, pineapple juice, olive oil, brown sugar, ginger powder, salt and cayenne pepper. Mix well.
2. Add marinade to a plastic baggie and add chicken breasts. Massage marinade into chicken lightly and seal. Refrigerate and marinate chicken at least 4 hours.
3. Heat a grill to medium heat.
4. Grill chicken breasts about 8-10 minutes, flipping once half way through, or until chicken is cooked through.
5. Remove from heat and chop. Set aside.
6. PEPPERS: Prepare your peppers by cutting off the top portion and scooping out the insides. Rinse.
7. Bring a large pot of water to boil. Boil the peppers about 4 minutes each to soften. Drain and set aside.
8. Preheat oven to 350 degrees.
9. Place peppers onto a lightly oiled deep baking dish. Stuff peppers with chopped chicken.
10. Bake 20-30 minutes, or until the peppers have softened.
11. FOR THE PINEAPPLE RELISH: Place pineapple into a large bowl and lightly mash. Remove pineapple into a mixing bowl and pour juice into a sauce pan.
12. Heat the pineapple juice to medium heat and add vinegar and sugar. Stir until sugar is dissolved. Remove from heat.
13. To mixing bowl with pineapple, add garlic, scallions and jalapeno peppers. Mix well.
14. Add juice, cilantro, salt and pepper to taste. Stir.
15. Remove peppers from heat and top each with the pineapple relish.
16. Serve!

California Burgers - Stuffed Pepper Style

California burgers are distinctive in that they are served with avocado and alfalfa sprouts. We've gone a step further and incorporated them into stuffed chili peppers. How's that for a variation? Same great taste with the added chili pepper bonus.

Ingredients

- 4 poblano peppers
- 2 jalapeno peppers, sliced
- 1 pound ground chuck
- 1 large avocado, sliced
- ½ cup alfalfa sprouts
- 8 ounces Pepper Jack cheese, shredded
- 1 small sweet onion, sliced
- Salt and pepper to taste

Cooking Directions

1. Roast the poblano peppers over an open flame, or use your oven broiler, until skins are blackened on each side. Over flame, it should only take about 5 minutes. In the broiler, it could take 10 or more minutes.
2. Remove poblano peppers and transfer to a plastic bag, and seal them up to let the skins loosen. Allow to cool.
3. Once cooled, peel off the blackened skins.
4. Slice each poblano pepper in half lengthwise and remove the innards with a knife or spoon.
5. Heat a large pan to medium heat and add ground chuck. Break apart with a wooden spoon while cooking and cook about 6 minutes, or until meat is nicely browned. Season with salt and pepper.
6. Preheat oven to 350 degrees.

7. Place poblano peppers onto a lightly oiled baking sheet and top each with ground chuck.
8. Bake 20 minutes.
9. Remove from heat and top with Pepper Jack cheese, jalapeno slices, avocado slices, onion slices and alfalfa sprouts.
10. Serve!

Random Tip

Holiday Thinking

Holidays are the perfect time to think about poppers and stuffed peppers. Jalapeno Poppers make for a tasty appetizer and are a sure crowd pleaser. Also, instead of serving up traditional holiday fare like ham or turkey, consider transforming those dishes into stuffed pepper recipes. Imagine - "Turkey and Stuffing Stuffed Poblanos with Gravy Sauce" or "Honey Glazed Ham Stuffed Cubanelles with Pineapple Topping".

Chicken Cordon Bleu Stuffed Peppers

Chicken Cordon Bleu is a simple yet tasty dish of chicken breast, flattened, then stuffed with a mixture of ham or other pork and a softer cheese. In this version, we've opted for cooked ham and a mixture of mozzarella and bleu cheese. Perfect for a stuffed pepper.

Ingredients

- 6 large poblano peppers or bell peppers
- 1 small onion, chopped
- 1 teaspoon garlic, minced
- 2 jalapeno peppers, finely chopped
- 2 tablespoons olive oil
- 2 tablespoon dried oregano
- 1 tablespoon dried basil
- 1 1/2 cups croutons, lightly crumbled
- 1/2 cup bread crumbs
- 1 cup cooked ham, chopped
- 1/2 cup mozzarella cheese
- 1/2 cup bleu cheese, crumbled
- 1 cup white rice, cooked
- 8 ounces tomato sauce
- 2 cups chicken breast, cooked and chopped
- Salt and pepper to taste

Cooking Directions

1. Prepare your peppers by cutting off the top portion and scooping out the insides. Rinse.
2. Heat a sauté pan to medium heat and add onion and jalapeno peppers with olive oil. Cook about 5 minutes to soften.
3. Add garlic and cook another minute. Add vegetables to a mixing bowl.

4. To mixing bowl, add oregano, basil, cooked chicken, ham, croutons, rice and bread crumbs.
5. Add tomato sauce with mozzarella and bleu cheese. Stir to combine, but do not over mix. NOTE: Your mixture should be the consistency of a stuffing. Add bread crumbs as needed.
6. Preheat oven to 350 degrees.
7. Stuff each pepper with your stuffing mixture and set onto a lightly oiled baking dish.
8. Bake 30-35 minutes.
9. Serve!

Black Bean and Rice Stuffed Bell Peppers

Get a dose of black beans with this vegetarian style stuffed pepper recipe. Beans have plenty of protein and they're smart to incorporate into a regular diet. We also call for salsa here. Try traditional style first, but after that, have fun with different salsa variations. Notes on that below. Get ready for the weekend!

Ingredients

- 6 large bell peppers
- 1 small onion, chopped
- 2 jalapeno peppers, chopped
- 2 tablespoons olive oil
- 1 teaspoon fresh garlic, minced
- 1 can of black beans
- 2 cups hot salsa
- 2 cups corn
- 1 1/2 cups brown rice
- 3 cups vegetable broth
- 1 teaspoon chili powder
- 1 teaspoon dried basil
- Salt and pepper to taste
- Fresh cilantro to taste

Cooking Directions

1. Prepare your peppers by cutting off the top portion and scooping out the insides. Rinse.
2. Heat a sauté pan to medium heat and add onion and jalapeno peppers with olive oil. Cook about 5 minutes to soften.
3. Add garlic and cook another minute.
4. Add vegetable broth and bring to a boil.

5. Add brown rice, chili powder and dried basil. Reduce heat to low and simmer until rice has absorbed the liquid, about 35-40 minutes.
6. Remove from heat and add corn, hot salsa and black beans. Add salt and pepper to taste.
7. Preheat oven to 350 degrees.
8. Stuff each pepper with your stuffing mixture and add pepper tops on top. Set onto a lightly oiled baking dish.
9. Top with aluminum foil and bake 30-35 minutes.
10. Top with fresh cilantro and serve!

Random Tip

Salsa Recipes

For fun salsa recipes that you can use for this recipe, visit http://www.chilipeppermadness.com or http://www.salsa-madness.com.

Orzo, Mushroom and Sausage Stuffed Peppers

Orzo is a rice-shaped pasta that lends itself nicely as a stuffing for peppers, especially when paired with flavor powerhouses like mushroom, sausage and Romano cheese. Fresh tomato is best for this recipe, though canned will work fine. Just be careful to not overdo the liquid with the canned variety.

Ingredients

- 6 large bell peppers
- 1-1/2 cups orzo
- 8 ounces Italian sausage
- 4-6 tomatoes, chopped
- 4 ounces mushrooms, chopped
- 6 ounces fresh Romano cheese, grated
- 1/4 cup olive oil
- 2 teaspoons fresh garlic, minced
- 4 cups chicken broth
- Salt and pepper to taste

Cooking Directions

1. Prepare your peppers by cutting off the top portion and scooping out the insides. Rinse.
2. Heat a sauté pan to medium and add sausage. Cook about 6-8 minutes, or until sausage is cooked through. Crumble and add to a mixing bowl and cool.
3. To mixing bowl, add chopped tomatoes, mushrooms, Romano cheese, olive oil, garlic, salt and pepper. Mix well.
4. Heat a large pot to medium heat and add chicken broth. Add orzo and cook about 5 minutes, until partially cooked.
5. Transfer orzo to mixing bowl and retain chicken broth. Mix well.
6. Preheat oven to 350 degrees.
7. Add about half of the chicken broth to a large, deep baking dish.
8. Stuff each pepper with your orzo-sausage-mushroom-cheese mixture. Place into the baking dish.
9. Cover baking dish with aluminum foil and bake about 30 minutes, or until peppers have softened.
10. Serve!

Poblanos Stuffed with Refried Beans and Cheddar

You don't need many ingredients for this stuffed pepper recipe. Refried beans are always in our cupboard so this recipe is easy to whip up in a hurry, which happens often for lunch when we're busy. We use cayenne pepper here, but spice it up even further with a habanero powder or diced fresh habanero peppers.

Ingredients

- 4 poblano peppers
- 16 ounces refried beans
- 1 cup cheddar cheese, shredded
- 1 small onion, minced
- 2 tablespoons taco seasonings
- 1 tablespoon cayenne pepper

Cooking Directions

1. Roast the poblano peppers over an open flame, or use your oven broiler, until skins are blackened on each side. Over flame, it should only take about 5 minutes. In the broiler, it could take 10 or more minutes.
2. Remove poblano peppers and transfer to a plastic bag, and seal them up to let the skins loosen. Allow to cool.
3. Once cooled, peel off the blackened skins.
4. Slice each poblano pepper in half lengthwise and remove the innards with a knife or spoon.
5. Preheat oven to 350 degrees.
6. In a large mixing bowl, combine refried beans, cheddar cheese, onion, cayenne and taco seasonings. Mix well.
7. Stuff each pepper half with your bean-cheese mixture and set onto lightly oiled baking sheets.
8. Bake 25-30 minutes.
9. Serve!

Salmon Stuffed Poblano Peppers Topped with Crab

We're huge salmon fans in the Madness household. It's a flavorful fish and easy to acquire where we live. It doesn't require a lot of seasoning, as we greatly enjoy the flavor of the fish, so we kept this recipe simple to focus on the salmon. The crab topping pairs nicely with it.

Ingredients

- 4 poblano peppers
- 8 ounces salmon sliced
- 4 ounces crab meat
- 4 ounces Romano cheese, shredded
- 2 tablespoons bread crumbs
- Olive oil
- 1 tablespoon lemon juice
- Salt and pepper to taste

Cooking Directions

1. Roast the poblano peppers over an open flame, or use your oven broiler, until skins are blackened on each side. Over flame, it should only take about 5 minutes. In the broiler, it could take 10 or more minutes.
2. Remove poblano peppers and transfer to a plastic bag, and seal them up to let the skins loosen. Allow to cool.
3. Once cooled, peel off the blackened skins.
4. Slice each poblano pepper in half lengthwise and remove the innards with a knife or spoon.
5. Set 2 ounces of salmon into each poblano pepper half. Drizzle lemon juice and olive oil over the tops of the salmon.
6. Season lightly with salt and pepper as desired.
7. Preheat oven to 350 degrees.

8. In a mixing bowl, combine crab meat, Romano cheese, bread crumbs, salt and pepper.
9. Top each salmon stuffed pepper with your crab meat mixture.
10. Set onto lightly oiled baking sheets and bake 20 minutes.
11. Serve!

Random Tip

Health Benefits of Chili Peppers

Chili peppers are good for you and smart to include in your daily diet. They are low in calorie, high in important vitamins, and offer a number of other benefits like fighting migraines, helping to lower blood pressure, helping you burn fat and lose weight, and more.

Visit www.chilipeppermadness.com for a list of other benefits.

Mac and Cheese Stuffed Peppers

An adult version of macaroni and cheese will work wonders for you. Sure, you can use the kid version, but it's so much more fun to make it from scratch and add in all the flavors you truly love. Here's a new spin on an old classic, stuffed into chili peppers.

Ingredients

- 4 bell peppers
- 2 cups elbow macaroni
- 4 teaspoons butter
- 1 cup Romano cheese, shredded
- 1 cup cheddar cheese, shredded
- 4 tablespoon heavy cream
- 2 teaspoons paprika
- 1 teaspoon cumin
- Salt and pepper to taste

Cooking Directions

1. Remove the stems from the peppers and remove seeds and innards.
2. Bring a large pot of water to boil and boil the peppers for 4 minutes to soften. Drain and set aside.
3. Prepare elbow macaroni as directed – basically, boil about 10 minutes until softened and drain.
4. Return cooked macaroni back to a pot and heat to medium heat. Add butter and stir until butter is melted.
5. Add heavy cream and cheeses. Stir constantly until cheeses are melted.
6. Remove from heat and add paprika, cumin, salt and pepper. Mix well.
7. Stuff each pepper with macaroni and cheese mixture and set onto lightly oiled baking dishes. Top with pepper tops.
8. Bake at 350 degrees 25-30 minutes.
9. Remove from heat and cool slightly before serving.

Crab Stuffed Peppers

Get yourself some lump crabmeat for this recipe, but if it's hard to come by or the price is too high for your tastes, any canned crab will work just fine. You can use most of these ingredients for a crab cake recipe, but we enjoy it stuffed into a chili pepper. Why? It's just so much more fun.

Ingredients

- 4 bell peppers
- 12 ounces crab meat
- ½ sweet onion, chopped
- 1 egg, beaten
- 1 cup bread crumbs
- ½ cup Romano cheese, shredded
- 1 teaspoon mustard powder
- 1 teaspoon dried parsley
- 1 teaspoon Worcestershire sauce
- Olive Oil

Cooking Directions

1. Remove the stems from the peppers and remove seeds and innards.
2. Bring a large pot of water to boil and boil the peppers for 4 minutes to soften. Drain and set aside.
3. Heat a sauté pan to medium heat and add onion with a splash of olive oil. Cook about 5 minutes to soften. Add to a large mixing bowl.
4. To mixing bowl, add crab meat, egg, bread crumbs, Romano cheese, mustard powder, dried parsley and Worcestershire sauce. Mix well.
5. Stuff each pepper with crab mixture and set onto a lightly oiled baking dish. Top with pepper tops.
6. Bake at 350 degrees 25-30 minutes.
7. Remove from heat and cool slightly before serving.

Chicken in Tomato Sauce Stuffed Peppers

This stuffed pepper recipe is best in the springtime when you have access to fresh basil direct from the garden. Fresh basil is so flavorful and distinctive, you'll crave it forever once you try it. Pair it with bacon in the tomato sauce and you have a meal that will make your tongue dance with pleasure.

Ingredients

- 4-6 bell peppers
- 2 pounds chicken breast, chopped
- 2 strips bacon, chopped
- 1 onion, chopped
- 16 ounces tomato sauce
- ½ cup fresh basil leaves, chopped
- Salt to taste
- Olive oil

Cooking Directions

1. Remove the stems from the peppers and remove seeds and innards.
2. Bring a large pot of water to boil and boil the peppers for 4 minutes to soften. Drain and set aside.
3. Heat a frying pan to medium heat and add chopped chicken breasts with about 1 teaspoon of olive oil. Season with salt. Cook 8 minutes, or until chicken slices are nicely browned. Set aside.
4. Heat a large pan to medium heat and add onion with chopped bacon slices. Cook about 5 minutes, or until onion is soft and bacon starts to crisp.
5. Add tomato sauce to pan and stir.
6. Add cooked chicken, basil and salt to taste. Mix well.
7. Stuff each pepper with chicken-tomato sauce mixture and set onto a lightly oiled baking dish. Top with pepper tops.
8. Bake at 350 degrees 25-30 minutes.
9. Remove from heat and cool slightly before serving.

Shrimp and Egg Stuffed Chili Peppers

This recipe is a spicy version of a frittata recipe we like to make for lazy Sunday brunches. It translates perfectly as a stuffing for chili peppers.

Ingredients

- 6 large sweet chili peppers
- 2 habanero peppers, chopped
- 12 ounces shrimp, peeled and deveined
- 8 ounces langoustines
- 4 ounces chopped spinach
- 6 eggs
- 4 ounces Jarlsberg cheese, shredded
- 2 tablespoons chili powder (or Cajun seasonings)
- Olive oil
- Salt and pepper to taste

Cooking Directions

1. Remove the stems from the peppers and slice them in half lengthwise.
2. Remove seeds and innards and discard.
3. Bring a large pot of water to boil and boil the peppers for 4 minutes to soften. Drain and set aside.
4. Heat a sauté pan to medium heat and lightly oil.
5. Roughly chop the shrimp and langoustines and sauté them about 2 minutes. Set aside.
6. Add spinach and habanero peppers to pan and cook until spinach is reduced, about 3 minutes. Remove from heat.
7. Set spinach and seafood mixture into a mixing bowl.
8. Beat eggs and pour into mixing bowl.
9. Add remaining ingredients to mixing bowl and mix well.
10. Set peppers onto a baking dish and fill each with equal amounts of egg-cheese mixture.
11. Bake at 350 degrees about 25-30 minutes, or until eggs are cooked through.
12. Remove from heat and allow to cool slightly before serving.

Apple Glazed Stuffed Peppers with Caramel Sauce

Dessert! You normally might not equate stuffed chili peppers with dessert, but it works. Especially if you are a chili pepper lover. Use tart green apples if you can find them, but any apple will work just fine. We like the tart ones as they bring a bit of a burst to the flavor profile here. Excellent for pairing with the simple caramel sauce.

Ingredients

- 4 bell peppers
- 8 small tart green apples, chopped
- 4 tablespoons butter
- 4 tablespoons brown sugar
- 1 teaspoon vanilla
- 1 teaspoon nutmeg
- 1 tablespoon cinnamon
- 2 teaspoons honey
- FOR THE CARAMEL SAUCE
- 1 cup sugar
- ¼ cup water
- ¼ teaspoon lemon juice
- ¾ cup heavy cream
- 2 tablespoons butter
- ½ teaspoon vanilla

Cooking Directions

1. Remove the stems from the peppers and remove seeds and innards. Slice peppers in half lengthwise.
2. Bring a large pot of water to boil and boil the peppers for 4 minutes to soften. Drain and set aside.

3. Heat a frying pan to medium heat and add chopped apples with butter.
4. Cook until butter is melted then add brown sugar. Cook about 1 minute.
5. Add vanilla, nutmeg, cinnamon and honey. Mix well and remove from heat.
6. Stuff each pepper with apple mixture and set onto a lightly oiled baking dish.
7. Bake at 350 degrees 25-30 minutes.
8. CARAMEL SAUCE
9. While the peppers are cooking, prepare your caramel sauce by adding sugar, water and lemon juice to a sauce pan. Stir to dissolve. Heat to medium-high heat and bring to a boil.
10. Cook about 5 minutes, swirling often, until the mixture turns to a dark amber color.
11. Add heavy cream. The mixture will bubble up and splatter a bit, so be careful.
12. Reduce heat and add butter. Mix continually until butter is melted and caramel achieves a nice consistency. Remove from heat.
13. Add vanilla and stir.
14. Remove stuffed peppers from oven. Pour caramel sauce into peppers and serve!

Random Tip

Chili Peppers for Dessert?

Absolutely! You can stuff your chili peppers with delicious sweetness. Also, consider candying some chili pepper slices and using them as a sweet topping for cakes and pies. Candied jalapeno peppers are quite popular.

Spicy Bumps
on a Pepper Log

Bumps on a log are a childhood tradition, so much so that you'll see that well into adulthood when the theme is fun and whimsical. We offer up our own spicy variation. You can easily whip these up at a moment's notice with very few ingredients.

Ingredients

- 10 serrano peppers
- 1 cup creamy peanut butter
- 1 tablespoon cayenne powder
- Raisins for topping

Cooking Directions

1. Remove stems from serrano peppers and slice them in half lengthwise.
2. Remove pepper innards and discard.
3. Spread peanut butter into the hollowed peppers.
4. Dust with cayenne pepper.
5. Top with raisins, about 4 or 5 raisins per pepper (these are your "bumps").
6. Serve!

NOTE: As a fun variation, use chocolate covered raisins instead.

Variations on Breading and Batters for Jalapeno Poppers and Stuffed Peppers

Most of our recipes call for a very simple bread crumb mixture for breading or a basic beer batter, but there are many, many ways you can coat your poppers and stuffed peppers before frying, baking, or grilling them. Feel free to substitute any of the breading instructions in the recipes with any of the following breading ideas...

Our Favorite Breading

A traditional chiles rellenos recipe calls for a very simple egg wash and a straightforward batter. This works not only for chiles rellenos, but for any jalapeno popper or stuffed pepper recipe. Here are the basic instructions:

Ingredients

- 2 eggs, separated
- ½ cup flour + ¼ cup, separated
- ½ cup milk
- Pinch of salt
- Pinch of baking powder
- Oil for frying

Cooking Directions

1. Prepare your stuffed peppers or jalapeno poppers.
2. Prepare your egg wash by beating the egg whites until stiff. Gently fold in the egg yolks and add to a bowl. The mixture will be light and fluffy.
3. Prepare your batter in a separate bowl by combining ½ cup flour with ½ cup milk, pinch of baking powder and pinch of salt.

4. Pour oil into a pan, about 1 to 1-1/2 inches deep, in order to cover half the stuffed peppers when you drop them in.
5. In one more bowl, add the ¼ cup dry flour.
6. Dip each pepper into the dry flour to coat each side. Then, dip into the egg mixture, then into the batter to coat completely. (As an alternative, you can combine the egg mixture and batter into one large batter and dip the peppers - try it as a variation).
7. Fry each pepper about 2-3 minutes each side, or until they are a golden brown. The batter should sizzle up immediately after placing the peppers into the oil.
8. Drain excess oil and serve!

Easy Beer Batter

Season 1 cup of flour with seasoned salt or other desired spices. Pour in one cup of beer. Mix well. Or, as another simple variation, stir in one egg yolk and only ¾ cup beer. If the batter is too thick add the remaining beer to thin the batter. Dip the jalapenos in the batter and fry, bake, or grill per recipe.

A Simple Breading

This combination works with anything, really, from chicken to fish, and of course, for poppers and stuffed peppers. Combine 1 cup flour, 1 cup breadcrumbs, 1 teaspoon chili powder or paprika, and a pinch each of salt and pepper. Add whatever other seasonings you prefer, such as garlic powder. Try dried basil for an Italian twist, or a bit of sugar for sweetness.

Pancake Mix

This one is super quick and works great if you have a box of dried pancake mix milling about your cupboard. Simply prepare the pancake mix per instructions in a mixing bowl. This usually consists of adding water to the mix. Dip the jalapenos in the batter and fry, bake, or grill per recipe.

Crushed Crackers

We don't necessarily recommend this particular breading variation, but it will work if you're stuck with no breadcrumbs and desperately need jalapeno poppers. Simply measure about 2 cups of crackers and process with a blender until finely chopped. Coat peppers with egg and coat with crackers, then prepare as needed. You can add as much seasoning to the crackers as desired.

Cornmeal

Cornmeal mixtures work great for jalapeno poppers. Substitute the following mixture for your breadcrumbs in any of the recipes.

- 1 cup cornmeal
- pinch of salt
- pinch of paprika
- pinch of onion powder
- pinch of garlic powder
- pinch of sugar

Basic Tempura Batter

Mix all of the following ingredients in a mixing bowl for your batter or breading. Add spices as desired. Get creative!

- 1 cup cornstarch
- 2 teaspoons baking powder
- 1 teaspoon baking soda
- ½ cup water
- 1 egg

Mix and Match and New Ideas

Another option is to mix and match as many of the above breading ideas to spice things up. For example, mix some dry cheese, such as grated Parmesan, into your breadcrumb mixture. Throw some breadcrumbs or crushed Gold Fish crackers into your cornmeal mix. Mix in some crushed tortilla chips. What about Panko, those Japanese bread crumbs? Feel free to experiment. That's the fun part of cooking!

Thank You

Thank you very much for enjoying your jalapeno poppers and stuffed chili peppers with us. We hope you've been able to try every recipe and have learned enough to experiment on your own with plenty of new ideas. With jalapeno poppers and other peppers, the stuffing possibilities are practically endless, limited only by your creativity. This collection was meant only to serve as the beginning of your popper journey. Live long and enjoy all of your chili peppers!

Copyright

Publisher's Note

Advice and information in this book are believed to be accurate and true at time of printing. The author cannot accept any legal responsibility or liability for any errors or omissions that might be made.

We did our best to ensure the accuracy of all recipes and measurements. As you know, cooking is often experimental and recipes might not always turn out exactly the same way twice. We certainly hope your recipes turn out as great as they did for us. We would have loved to include photos for all our recipes, but cost was a factor. You can, however, see some of these online at www.JalapenoMadness.com in the recipes section, at www.ChiliPepperMadness.com and also on our Facebook Fan Page at www.facebook.com/ChiliPepperMadness.

About the Author

Mike Hultquist is a strange yet devoted Jalapeño and Chili Pepper Lover trying to spread the word about spicy food. His focus is on home cooking and making every day meals spicy and fun. You can visit his web sites at

- http://www.jalapenomadness.com
- http://www.chilipeppermadness.com
- http://www.habaneromadness.com

He is also a fiction writer and screenwriter. You can learn more about Mike's works at **http://www.michaelhultquist.com**.